TRANSFORM
and
THRIVE

DOROTHY STOLTZ

with Gail Griffith, James Kelly, Muffie Smith, and Lynn Wheeler

TRANSFORM *and* THRIVE

IDEAS to *Invigorate*
Your Library and Your Community

ALA
Editions

CHICAGO 2018

DOROTHY STOLTZ is director for community engagement at the Carroll County (MD) Public Library. She is the coauthor of several books and articles for the American Library Association, including *Inspired Collaboration: Ideas for Discovering and Applying Your Potential* (2016). With more than thirty-five years of experience in public libraries, she is active in the Library Leadership & Management Association, the Public Library Association, and the Association for Library Service to Children.

Extensive effort has gone into ensuring the reliability of the information in this book; however, the publisher makes no warranty, express or implied, with respect to the material contained herein.

ISBN: 978-0-8389-1622-3 (paper)

Library of Congress Cataloging-in-Publication Data

Names: Stoltz, Dorothy, author. | Griffith, Gail, author. | Kelly, James (Librarian), author. | Smith, Muffie, author. | Wheeler, Lynn, author.

Title: Transform and thrive : ideas to invigorate your library and your community / Dorothy Stoltz ; with Gail Griffith, James Kelly, Muffie Smith, and Lynn Wheeler.

Description: Chicago : ALA Editions, an imprint of the American Library Association, 2018. | Includes bibliographical references and index.

Identifiers: LCCN 2018001086 | ISBN 9780838916223 (paper : alk. paper)

Subjects: LCSH: Library personnel management. | Libraries and community.

Classification: LCC Z682 .S837 2018 | DDC 023—dc23 LC record available at https://lccn.loc.gov/2018001086

Cover design by Krista Joy Johnson. Book composition by Alejandra Diaz in the Freight Text Pro and BentonSans typefaces.

♾ This paper meets the requirements of ANSI/NISO Z39.48–1992 (Permanence of Paper).

Printed in the United States of America

22 21 20 19 18   5 4 3 2 1

For Adreon
~Dorothy~

For K and Mo, with all my love
~J~

For Sammy and Maggie
who have taught me so much
~Muffie~

CONTENTS

PREFACE

Children pay little attention to the color of the exterior of the bookmobile. They climb up the steps at every visit to find a treasure trove inside of books, ideas, and endless learning. The bookmobile librarian, a sweet, kind young staffer, seems a combination comedian, scholar, and champion of all that's good in the world. The bookmobile is essential because rural areas, devoid of a library, may require a car or other transportation to reach the closest library building.

This portrait is as typical today in many communities as it was years ago—in rural, suburban, and metropolitan areas throughout the country.

Given modern technology, we have easy access to information at our fingertips. Anyone can research, learn, and discover ideas virtually anytime and anywhere using computers of all shapes and sizes. Why should a community support a library? What's the benefit for a community-at-large to fund a public library in its geographic locale? Andrew Trexler, engineer and designer with Catalyst Space, challenged a group of librarians: "Since people can now hold the information world literally in their hand with a small device, what are libraries doing to survive and thrive?" Perhaps we in the library profession have just been assuming all along that libraries are worthwhile and contribute to society. But the times are changing.

Are libraries like a dinosaur of the past heading for extinction? Are libraries undergoing a downgrade in the minds of the public, like Pluto's downgrade in status from a planet to a dwarf planet? It may be folly to propose that every community will fund, or continue to fund a library. Do we have to propose radical solutions, such as closing down the library?

This book will debunk the notion that libraries are coming to the end of their usefulness as public institutions. In fact, this book will present a series of tenets for right understanding and right action to awaken you to creating new roles for librarians. It suggests ideas for you to ponder as you try to help your community be its best. How can the modern library thrive? How can the modern library master staying in touch with the pulse of the community? How can the library weave a tapestry of whatever is good for the community?

Because of the generosity and genius of Andrew Carnegie, businessman and philanthropist, public libraries were reinvented in the late nineteenth and early twentieth centuries. The public library, however, has become more than the Carnegie Library of the past. It has *grown!* Librarians who are not geared toward change create an environment in which a library may atrophy over time. When people vote on whether to support their local library through a mill levy, for example, they may actually be voting on their childhood memory of the library. It is incumbent upon library staffers not to try to relive the glory days of the past.

In order to grapple with change versus the status quo, library staff members should recognize that the library is an institution that is alive, expanding, and developing. This book celebrates the human drive to learn, grow, and flourish. Rapid change is not necessarily desirable, but an unwillingness to change is equally unhelpful. Libraries need to reconcile these differences and strive for a harmonious approach.

Aristotle called the ideal harmony between two extremes the golden mean. "Concerning . . . pleasantness in life, the one who is pleasant in a way one ought to be is friendly and the mean condition is friendliness, the one who goes to excess, if it is for no purpose, is obsequious, but if it is for his own advantage, he is a flatterer, and the one who falls short and is unpleasant in everything is a certain sort of contrary person, and hard to get along with."[1] (You can find this quote and more insights about the golden mean in *Aristotle Nicomachean Ethics* in your library.)

Aristotle describes three tendencies or frames of mind: two of them are unsound, one resulting from excess and the other from insufficiency, and the third of them he calls a virtue. This virtue or condition of excellence is the mean condition or the golden mean. The extremes are not only opposite to each other but opposite to the mean condition. For example, "the courageous person appears rash in relation to the coward and cowardly in relation to the rash person, and similarly . . . the generous person appears wasteful in relation to the stingy person and stingy in relation to the wasteful person." It takes work to establish a balance in life. Libraries that strive for the golden mean are developing tenets of how to produce excellent service that grows, expands, and develops. This work is not easy, but it is worthwhile and should be celebrated. As Aristotle said, work that aims at the mean is work well done and is "praiseworthy and beautiful."[2]

What works well in public libraries? What can we do differently to be more effective? What is the new role of a library? Let's celebrate our libraries. Let's celebrate library staffers—like the kind, fun, and smart young bookmobile librarian who tells all ages to strive to be their best and think for themselves. Let's celebrate the ultimate human resource—thinking! Let's celebrate our communities—no matter what their starting point! We can develop ways to bring out the best in library staff members in order to better serve a community. For instance, if those working in a library demonstrate competence, cheerfulness, and respect for all, the library can spark curiosity and encourage the good in the community. As Ralph Waldo Emerson said, "There is no beautifier of complexion, or form, or behavior, like the wish to *scatter* joy and not pain around us."[3] Libraries can *scatter joy* as a baseline in order to play an important role in helping a community flourish.

However, if a library leader does not think things through, he or she may end up like King Richard the Second in Shakespeare's play *Richard II*,

> Down, down I come; like glistering Phaethon,
> Wanting the manage of unruly jades.
> In the base court? Base court, where kings grow base,
> To come at traitors' calls and do them grace.
> In the base court? Come down? Down, court!
> down, king!
> For night-owls shriek where mounting larks
> should sing.

Even though King Richard the Second may not have thought things through—as a character in the play—the question remains: is your library squandering its opportunity to help your community be its best?

This book will offer ideas and tenets to study, digest, and ponder. If you do so, you may help your community sing like the lark in John Masefield's poem *The Everlasting Mercy*:

> By this the sun was all one glitter,
> The little birds were all atwitter;
> Out of a tuft a little lark
> Went higher up than I could mark,

His little throat was all one thirst
To sing until his heart should burst
To sing aloft in golden light
His song from blue air out of sight.

The Everlasting Mercy is a poem of transformation from something relatively unpolished and incomplete to someone reaching his or her potential. Libraries can strive for a balanced approach—the golden mean—as a way to reach their potential and thrive. Join us, the authors, on a journey to explore the tenets of right librarianship for the next century and beyond.

NOTES

1. Aristotle, *Aristotle Nicomachean Ethics,* ed. and trans. Joe Sachs (Newburyport, MA: Focus/R. Pullins, 2002), 32.

2. Aristotle, *Aristotle Nicomachean Ethics*, 32–35.

3. Ralph Waldo Emerson, *The Conduct of Life* (1860, rev. 1876), www.emersoncentral .com/behavior.htm.

ACKNOWLEDGMENTS

We would like to thank the many wise, gracious, and helpful people inside and outside libraries who shared their ideas for invigorating libraries and communities, especially the inspiring folk at the Carroll County Public Library, in Maryland libraries generally, and the many thoughtful colleagues we've met through the Public Library Association, the Library Leadership & Management Association, the Association for Library Services to Children, and the ALA's Program Office.

Special thanks to the ALA president Sarah Long (1999–2000) for her inspiration, insights, and support for this project—and for helping to transform librarianship at the turn of the millennium.

Special thanks to the dedicated staff at the Folger Shakespeare Library, Library of Congress, the Library Company of Philadelphia, Chicago Public Library, Pioneer Library System of Canandaigua (NY), Rochester (NY) Regional Library District, New York Public Library, Cleveland Public Library, Montana State Library, Pennsylvania State Library, and the gems in our backyard, the Maryland State Library Agency, the Enoch Pratt Free Public Library, and the Maryland State Library Resource Center.

With appreciation for ongoing insights from those helping to transform libraries and communities at the ALA's Center for the Future of Libraries, the Aspen Institute, Erikson Institute, Future Ready Librarians, Harwood Institute of Public Innovation, New America, Global Family Research, WQED-PBS Pittsburgh, and many other great explorers.

We'd like to express gratitude and celebrate Jamie Santoro and all the superb folks at ALA Editions.

INTRODUCTION

With several nods to Charles Dickens—enough to keep one's head bobbing—libraries exist today in "the best of times and the worst of times." According to modern research, while most Americans think that libraries offer lifelong learning opportunities for all ages that benefit their communities, many people remain unaware of specific programs and services at their local library. This is the age of wisdom and the age of foolishness. Some libraries consistently ask what's working, what's not, and what they can do differently in order to be more effective, while other libraries just think about how to get more money. Depending on library leadership, it can be a season of light for some libraries or a season of darkness for others. It can be the spring of hope and the winter of despair at the same time—if a library serves 150 teens after school lets out in the afternoon but doesn't have a plan to serve them wisely.[1]

Strongly influenced by Benjamin Franklin, Dorothy Stoltz directs community engagement, programming, and outreach for a public library and salutes the habit of thinking things through. Gail Griffith, who worked for many years as a deputy library director and then moved into consulting, relishes strategic organizational change and makes decision-making a delight. As a library administrator and the father of a young daughter, James Kelly connects people to ideas and, ultimately, to each other, whether linking librarians to useful ideas inside and outside the profession or his daughter to the joys of Zachariah OHora's *No Fits, Nilson!* Muffie Smith, a library human resources director, creates high-performing teams, encourages all to apply their individual potential, and treasures a good sense of humor while helping an organization sparkle. The library executive director Lynn Wheeler illuminates the thinking of elected officials and community stakeholders in ways that can expand the library's power to support human growth and help a community shine.

This book will offer key tenets to help any size library—no matter what its level of funding—to improve and thrive. The book is divided into four sections:

I. Developing a culture where groupthink is reduced, learning—and unlearning—are encouraged, and intelligent risk-taking is valued.
II. Pondering library customer service concepts of respect and goodwill and why going above and beyond the call of duty will be standard in libraries of the future.
III. Leading from any position to practice integrity, grace, and patience and transform the library from a book repository into a community anchor by finding treasures in your stacks to uplift humanity.
IV. Refreshing our minds and activating creativity in order to avoid getting stuck in the past and to appropriately and effectively respond to any problem, challenge, or barrier and bring out the genius—or inner best—of everyone.

This book is aimed at readers who have a deep interest in seeing libraries evolve and flourish. It should also appeal to readers with a professional—and personal—interest in learning to think completely in order to uplift humanity through library services and activities. Take the time to reflect on the ideas presented in this book. *Transform and Thrive* is an attempt to reawaken the library profession and nourish its growth for years to come.

NOTE

1. Charles Dickens, *A Tale of Two Cities* (1859; New York: Barnes & Noble, 1993), 1.

PART I

RISK-TAKING

One

STARTLE YOURSELF

*A chief event of life is the day
in which we have encountered a mind that startled us.*

RALPH WALDO EMERSON

"All for one and one for all," group norms, and crowd-sourcing are management and team tools that create loyalty, enhance a safe environment for discussion and decision-making, and can bring outside ideas to the table. If not used wisely, however, these kinds of tools can also lead to groupthink, follow the crowd, or comfort-of-the-herd-type thinking in your work. It's easy to adopt a crowd mentality, especially because the rule of many is an important feature in a democracy. The first known democracy, however—in ancient Greece—was the same society that turned to mob rule and condemned Socrates to death. Socrates was known to expose the specious arrogance of the "wisdom" of Athenian elders. He startled people regularly. For example, he was falsely accused of corrupting youth—by asking questions and encouraging people to think things through.[1]

In growing up we may not have learned to think in this way—to startle ourselves and others by challenging accepted beliefs. Reading about the death sentence of Socrates may make us think, "Tut tut, that was uncalled for." However, the execution of Socrates served to startle Western society. "Decisions made by many are sometimes superior, but when the many lack expertise, are biased in one particular direction, or gravitate towards an appealing but incorrect alternative, the crowd's decisions turn out to be more foolish than the individual's decisions," says Adam Alter, assistant professor of marketing at New York University's Stern School of Business.[2]

Have you ever walked into a meeting where most of those assembled align with a groupthink mentality? It sometimes takes considerable skill to introduce an idea or concept that will startle those around the table in order to break up the follow-the-crowd syndrome. This is different than playing "devil's advocate," which has its place as long as it is not overplayed.

Abraham Lincoln is an example of someone who was able to think for himself on a regular basis and break up incidents of groupthink. Shortly before his first inauguration, Lincoln stunned a group of New York City merchants by his political genius. As supporters—and deputies—of New York Senator William Seward's quest to become part of the president's cabinet, they protested Lincoln's choice to include Seward's antagonist, the Ohio governor Salmon Chase, in the cabinet.

Lincoln unveiled two lists of names to the merchants that revealed his thinking and made a point. The first list reflected his preferred choice of cabinet members, with the names of Chase as treasury secretary and Seward as secretary of state. This list meant that Seward would be compelled to act as a team player in order to be appointed to the cabinet. The second list reflected a poorer choice, as Lincoln described it, with Chase as treasurer and New Jersey Senator William Dayton as secretary of state. The group left the room in silence.

Once a stunning or startling idea is introduced at a meeting, the discussion has the *potential* of turning into a higher level of give-and-take. Problems can be more easily resolved if the higher level of discussion can be maintained. The meeting can move in a more dynamic, provocative, and productive direction. It is like opening a window in order to see—and understand— that new possibilities lie ahead. Or in the Lincoln example, the meeting breaks up, allowing the president—or a library director, or a CEO, or some other leader—to get back to the important business of creative thinking and decision-making.

CREATIVITY

Edward de Bono, author, trainer, and a leading authority on creative thinking, developed the concept of lateral thinking in the late 1960s. In this pursuit of wisdom, a person opens up his or her mind and explores possibilities. This creativity is not about playing the piano or painting landscapes, or even about designing what a robot can do. "For the first time in human history we can treat creativity as a mental skill, not just a matter of talent or inspiration,"[3] says de Bono.

Lateral or creative thinking is about challenging your assumptions. It's about sparking curiosity in yourself and others. How many alternative ways of thinking can you generate—exploring up, down, and sideways before moving forward? Lateral thinking is not about narrowing your focus in order to find the first promising answer; instead, it keeps asking "What is possible?" even after a promising answer appears. It is not brainstorming or brainwriting. You may hear this concept called provocative thinking, or ideation, or the Six Thinking Hats—an exercise designed by de Bono—or serendipitous discovery . . . or just wondering "Hmmm, what's the ideal and how can I implement it?" De Bono says, "Our culture and habits of thinking insist that we always move towards certainty. We need to pay attention to possibility . . . [It's] the key to creativity."[4]

The word "startle" gives us the sense of moving suddenly in surprise, according to early definitions dating back to the 1520s. It is related to the word "start," which goes back further to the Proto-Indo-European root *ster*, which means "stiff." "Stiff" can be traced back to the Old Norse language word *stifla*, or "choke." The television character Archie Bunker tells his wife, Edith, in *All in the Family*, to "stifle." Archie is telling Edith, "Stop what you are saying," and implies, "Stop what you are thinking." Many people may not have agreed with Archie's views on the world, but he certainly startled people to challenge their assumptions.

"Leading the examined life," as Socrates described it, can inspire the library as an organization to cultivate a creative, reliable, and compelling service environment. In order to do this, we must be willing to startle ourselves. By examining what works and what doesn't work on a regular basis, a library can tap the strength of an orderly and poised process for startling decision-making. We need to employ unexpected new developments and new ideas. When a library creates a learning philosophy, in which each employee is responsible for his or her own learning, it can connect staff members to the library's goal of supporting human growth. A library's self-discipline to grow and learn as an organization in order to serve its community magnifies the possibilities and the opportunities to be able to do so.[5]

WAKE UP!

As adults we may not have been asked to think on this higher level of lateral or creative thinking since high school or college—or ever. Startling ourselves and others with new thinking and new ideas is not meant to shock, but to wake up the library field and the communities we serve. One way to wake up our library organization and community is by consistently offering top-notch service. We make the effort to express excellence in what we do. It doesn't matter what the level of library funding is, or staffing, or size of space. The people working in a library determine whether the service will be adequate, or good, or top-notch. All libraries can figure out what their community members need and will respond to by engaging in conversations with residents, students, businesses, and families—and trying things out.

The following chart compares "adequate to good" service vs. "top-notch" service when focusing on library programs, events, and activities.

Service	Adequate to Good	Top-Notch (in addition to the qualities in the previous column)
Programming	▪ Library provides a standard set of programs for a variety of age groups: storytimes, book clubs, crafts—whatever the librarians know about or might learn about ▪ Programs are advertised using a standard set of sources: library news releases, social media, website, and newsletter ▪ Library uses a teen advisory board to help develop programs	▪ Startling people in order to shake them out of their traditions. ▪ Staff proactively figure out what the community needs or will respond to, and develop the skills or connections to provide programs on these topics, in whatever languages are needed; for example, discussion forums, classic literature book clubs, reading contests, author events, Shakespeare workshops. ▪ Staff collaborate with partner organizations to jointly develop and/or cross-promote programs. ▪ Staff at all levels promote the library's programs; for example, circulation staff inform—without badgering—people at checkout about an upcoming program relevant to them. ▪ Staff intentionally develop new skills in order to startle the community with programs in emerging areas or by upping the ante in existing areas of interest. For example, staff might learn about robotics, puppetry, or opera in order to offer a program.

Examining the topic of food can demonstrate examples of top-notch library programs. Crown Finish Caves, a cheese aging and distribution center, is located inside a nineteenth-century, 30-foot-deep tunnel in Crown Heights, Brooklyn. The Brooklyn Public Library features artisans and entrepreneurs such as Crown Finish Caves in the library's annual program series called "Created in Brooklyn." Randy Duchaine, a photographer, is the program's host, and he interviews the borough's artists and innovators whom he captures in his photos. "People come to Brooklyn to live their dreams, express themselves, start a business, and contribute to society through their talents. They represent the spirit of America, a sense of independence, and the ability to stand on their own two feet and proudly say: This is what it means to be an American in Brooklyn," says Duchaine. His photograph exhibits and discussion programs at the library engage and inspire excellence.

Teams of teenagers face off against one another in a program based on the *Food Network* television show where two chefs face off making dishes centered on a secret ingredient. Katie Boyer, head of teen services at the Benton Harbor (MI) Public Library, facilitates culinary-related programs. Teens can learn about the value of teamwork, creative thinking, and maintaining cheerfulness despite a "win or lose" outcome.

"Expanding their curriculum in ever-innovative ways, public libraries are experimenting with installing professional kitchens, teaching cooking classes, and other food-related activities for students of all ages," says Valerie Gross, author and president and CEO of the Howard County (MD) Library System. For example, "Chow Down on Wellness" classes at the Culinary Literacy Center at the Free Library of Philadelphia teach how to cook a delicious and healthy dish while providing the opportunity for creative self-expression, friendship, and delight.

- Am I truly doing what's best for the library, or am I just defending worn-out traditions?
- How can I develop a healthy curiosity in order to gently, firmly, and consistently challenge traditions?
- How can I startle myself each day to choose possibility in my thinking rather than certainty?
- What steps can my library take to move from an adequate program to a top-notch program?

FIGURE 1.1

New York Times best-selling author and seventh-generation farmer Forrest Pritchard appeared at the Howard County (MD) Library System (HCLS) in October 2016 to discuss his farm and the challenges faced by today's small farmers. Pritchard was the inaugural guest of HCLS's podcast, HiJinx, in September, which also featured John Dove, a local farmer and owner of Love Dove Farms, and Joe and Mary Barbera, owners of Aida Bistro, who have built their restaurant around the farm-to-table concept. Participants learn about and are inspired by farming, food, and entrepreneurial ventures.

Photo: Courtesy of Howard County (MD) Library System

FIGURE 1.2

A young library patron follows the cookie recipe during a preschooler cooking lesson activity. In the process, children learn about the value of measurement, the value of ratios, patience as the cookies bake, and the joy of cooking.

Photo: Courtesy of Carroll County (MD) Public Library

Librarians (and everyone working in a library) can be described as experimenters of how to enlighten humanity. How can libraries offer programs that will startle, inspire, and spark curiosity? The sky is the limit when it comes to connecting people to library programs and services. As Emerson said, "Be real and admirable, not as we know, but as you know. Able men do not care in what kind a man is able, so only that he is able. A master likes a master, and does not stipulate whether it be orator, artist, craftsman, or king."[6] Let's be experimenters, collaborators, and masters of all things "library." We have a serious responsibility to our communities. Let's startle ourselves and the people we serve with common sense, our respect for others, and our ability to celebrate all that's good in our community.

NOTES

1. Dorothy Stoltz et al., *Inspired Collaboration: Ideas for Discovering and Tapping Your Potential* (Chicago: American Library Association, 2016), 10.
2. Psychology Today, https://www.psychologytoday.com/basics/groupthink.
3. Edward de Bono, *Creativity Workout: 62 Exercises to Unlock Your Most Creative Ideas* (Berkeley, CA: Ulysses, 2008), 16.
4. De Bono, *Creativity Workout*, 8.
5. Stoltz et al., *Inspired Collaboration*, 10.
6. EmersonCentral.com, http://emersoncentral.com/goethe.htm.

Two

LEARNING THE RIGHT THINGS

Discern with a painter's eye to look at the laws about beauty,
goodness, justice . . . and to guard and preserve them.

PLATO, *THE REPUBLIC, BOOK VI*

Values are sculpted by the mind and establish a foundation for inner strength—no matter if one's emotions are sad or happy, irritated or calm. A value is something we treasure, cultivate, and watch over, consciously or unconsciously. We are motivated by our values to invest time, energy, and resources. Respect for others, innovation, and embracing change reflect core values in top-notch library organizations, but we should not stop there. The ability to recognize and implement important values in order to benefit the work at hand—such as risk-taking, quality, and humor—helps a library invigorate itself and the community it serves.

It is not necessary to be constantly thinking about or discussing values. The idea is to live within a framework of core values that moves the organization into the future in successful ways. Examining the results of your library services and activities—what's working and what's not—can be an excellent reflection tool to determine success, and it can also be a keen reminder of your values. For example, Denise strengthened her library's partnerships with the boys and girls club and a local school because she was not only willing to take new and emerging technology activities to their buildings, but led students in learning to use technology—as she was learning too. Although Denise studied the technology and learned to use it, she clearly stepped out of her area of expertise. Yet, she willingly—and cheerfully—made mistakes

FIGURE 2.1

Lifelong learning for both students and librarian using Cubelets and Ozobots.

Photo: Courtesy of Carroll County (MD) Public Library

during the hands-on experience as she facilitated the activities. She was not only open to learning from the students, but actually encouraged them to teach her and each other as they quickly caught on to the fun technology. "We're figuring this out together!" Denise put a core value—perhaps without realizing it—into action. She implemented the "love of learning" and embraced the idea of lifelong learning.

But what is learning? Are we learning the right things and applying them in our daily work? Are we learning how to spend an inordinate amount of time putting out small fires? Or do we have a balanced approach and spend time on what Stephen Covey, author of *The Seven Habits of Highly Effective People*, called "important but not urgent" activities—activities such as relationship-building, prevention, and recognizing new opportunities. Denise pondered her outreach opportunities and pursued relationship building with the boys and girls club. She worked closely with the club director and her staff, facilitated activities at their location, sponsored a pop-up maker lab, and presented at their annual gala dinner about how fun technology can be for everyone of all ages—including herself. The result: she reached hundreds of new students who normally don't use the library, and she laid the foundation to bolster the collaboration.

Learning is more than acquiring knowledge and experience, memorizing facts and figures, gaining comprehension and skills, and becoming aware and informed. It is the thoughtful study, understanding, and ability to integrate into our self what is needed to ask the right questions, be creative, and produce worthwhile results. It is the process that converts knowledge into wisdom.

The right kind of learning results in the ability of library staffers to spark curiosity in ways that cultivate their own self-initiated learning. They create communities of practice around specific topics or learning communities. *Staff members bolster their inquisitiveness, cherish wisdom, and apply practical knowledge to fulfill the director's vision.*

If the library profession ignores the potential of new and emerging technology to enhance its work and to support library patrons so they can benefit from these technologies, many libraries will quickly become obsolete. If libraries make programming, collection, and service decisions without asking the people they serve questions—such as "What more can the library do for you?"—many libraries will become ineffective. Without library staffers regularly asking questions, library services will be designed in a vacuum. Without staffers developing a curiosity about what more they can do to support their community, why will a community support the library?

FIGURE 2.2

Trying a virtual rock-climbing game may help some people overcome a fear of heights, thus letting them clean their houses' rain gutters. The game can be a trial run for others who are interested in training for a real climb.

Photo: Courtesy of Talbot County (MD) Public Library

FIGURE 2.3

National Park Service rangers talked with students about the types of fossils typically found in the C & O Canal National Historic Park and what those fossils tell us about our distant past. Students examined real fossils collected in the park system and then created their own fossils with clay and shells.

Photo: Courtesy of Allegany County (MD) Public Library

"The right thing is . . . to value every customer and realize the importance of each in building [programs and services.] Your appreciation of your customers and focus on delivering value to them are a prerequisite to customer satisfaction, growth, and success," says Martin Zwilling, founder and CEO of Startup Professionals.[1]

UNLEARNING

A key to learning is "unlearning." The notion that the world was flat or was a disk floating in the ocean is found throughout ancient history. The voyages of the Norse, Columbus, and others helped break the unnecessary panic of sailors who mistakenly believed they would fall off the edge of a flat earth. Together, humanity unlearned this irrational fear.

What do you fear?

Do you ask questions as a way to examine what needs unlearning in your library? Questions such as:

- Is learning something that is pedagogical? Does it have to be tied to a specific curriculum and taught by a teacher? Or is the library designed for people of all ages to learn just about anything without someone saying learn this and learn that? Unlearn!
- Were you taught that it takes too much time to collaborate with colleagues or community partners, and you therefore miss the benefit of synergy? Unlearn!
- Did you learn as a child that play is frivolous, and therefore doesn't belong in libraries? Did you learn that "silence" rules everything in a library, and

therefore libraries cannot offer spaces for children to play and express their joy of learning? Unlearn!

- Have you been coached to view brainstorming sessions as the best way to seek input and find the "one" best solution to a challenge, and therefore you never focus on other ways to get broader input and arrive at multiple best solutions? Unlearn!
- Did you learn as a supervisor that clerical staff members should never interact with patrons in a way that resembles the duties of a "professional librarian," and consequently the library misses an opportunity for a clerical staffer to offer a program on learning to paint with watercolors or to listen and respond to a patron who has a great idea for a new service? Unlearn!

STRIVING FOR THE IDEAL

Plato describes "good play" among children as that which leads to the good. He contrasts it with "bad play," which deflects the learner from this goal. Children who learn how to play in an ideal spirit and develop a habit of playing together in pursuit of the "good" are more likely to grow up with playful and inquisitive minds.

Did you study Plato's *The Republic* in high school or college? Book VII or "The Allegory of the Cave" can help you ponder how to serve the community. The allegory reflects on how to think beyond the mundane details of life, to expand your vision to see the forest beyond the trees—or the sunlight beyond the cave. Part of the benefit of the allegory is that it demonstrates the value of unlearning. The people who are chained to a bench in a cave need to unlearn that the shadows on the cave's wall are reality. They need to learn that life outside the cave is the source of reality.

Socrates leads Glaucon, Plato's brother, in a dialogue to think in terms of the big picture about the role of the individual: strive to bring out the best in yourself and others. Those who do not have a sense of commitment to themselves or their community or those who do not act for the greater good will not take on this role in life. How can libraries offer opportunities for people to get excited about what interests them, become enthusiastic about learning, and achieve a high level of motivation to act and be productive? How can libraries help people learn to think things through, recognize what's true or false in life, and strive to be their best for the community?

FIGURE 2.4

Curious George and the Man in the Yellow Hat visit a storytime to help spark curiosity and encourage Plato's idea of "good play."

Photo: Courtesy of South Butler (PA) Community Library and WQED-PBS Pittsburgh

Plato's *Theaetetus* contains another allegory using the Socratic dialogue technique. It helps us examine the role of the mind in discerning truth and falsehood. Socrates leads Theaetetus, a mathematician, in a delightful discussion in which he asks "What is knowledge?" and ponders the difference between "possessing" and "having" knowledge. If the weather is such that you leave your coat at home when you step outside, you do not "have" your coat (with you), yet you "possess" a coat. The line of thinking that follows is that you can possess knowledge and still not have it, that is, not use it.

Socrates asks more questions that encourage the reader to ponder and think about life skills; for example, do you believe a thing to be true because your friends believe it? Have you acquired a set of assumptions or a system of beliefs that no longer work? Socrates describes the importance of pondering and discerning what is true and what is not by likening the mind to an aviary.

In the dialogue, Socrates posits a person who hunts and captures many birds of all types from lots of places to make an aviary at home to take care of them. Or a person could acquire an entire flock of birds from one specific source. These birds may be wrens or doves or other kinds of birds, common or rare, and these birds are like pieces of knowledge or pieces of ignorance flying around individually or in small or large groups in the aviary (the mind).

As Socrates says to Theaetetus, "There are two phases of hunting; one before you have possession in order to get possession, and another when you already possess in order to catch and have in your hands what you previously acquired."[2] Are there too many birds—too much knowledge or not the right kind of knowledge? Does the aviary owner spend time correctly identifying and getting to "know" the birds? What true-false criteria are used to identify and appreciate the birds?

Socrates encourages a deliberate selection of birds (select knowledge or truth over ignorance or falsehood), a nurturing environment or aviary (develop a playful and mature mind), and a method to identify the species and the beauty and potential of each bird (discernment to identify whether an idea or piece of knowledge is worthwhile and how to make good use of it).

In these ways Library ABC will be empowered to make decisions that are right for its community and not based on what Library XYZ is doing or has done. It's helpful to be inspired by ideas from other libraries, but it's important to be discerning and respond to individuals and groups within *your* community. Can library leadership and staff members develop programs and services based on what's working in their community, as opposed to always taking a cookie-cutter approach to library service based on a library in the next county or state? At the same time, it can be helpful from time to time to replicate what another library is doing as a means to quickly jump-start a service or program, and then modify it to fit the community.

This role of the mind—to discern truth and falsehood—gives us a fresh perspective on a library's core value of "we each are responsible for our own learning." Each library staffer is responsible for analyzing successfully whether the excitement in the room accurately reflects an intelligent project design, for example, or for thinking independently from what one's favorite blogger is saying. "The key to using technology in a program, for example, is to incorporate it in a thoughtful and engaging way that utilizes a particular platform to achieve specific goals—not to add it on superficially," says Robert Forloney, professor, museum consultant, and library board trustee. How can you learn to sift through ideas to determine those that will or will not work in the long run? How can you develop organizational values to bring out the best in your thinking and decision-making? How can you learn to generate not one or two good ideas, but ten or twenty or a hundred great ideas per project? What can you do to learn the right things in order to produce long-term results?

The importance of values, such as the fact that we're each responsible for our own learning—and unlearning—cannot be overstated. Benjamin Franklin established a "library company" in Philadelphia in 1731 to encourage book lending beyond a group of friends. In the late nineteenth and early twentieth centuries, Andrew Carnegie donated millions of dollars to establish libraries

SOCRATES: Now look here: is it possible in this way to possess knowledge and not "have" it? Suppose a man were to hunt wild birds, pigeons or something, and make an aviary for them at his house and look after them there; then, in a sense, I suppose, we might say he "has" them all the time, because of course he possesses them. Isn't that so?

THEAETETUS: Yes.

SOCRATES: But in another sense he "has" none of them; it is only that he has acquired a certain power in respect of them, because he has got them under his control in an enclosure of his own. That is to say, he has the power to hunt for any one he likes at any time, and take and "have" it whenever he chooses, and let it go again; and this he can do as often as he likes.

THEAETETUS: That is so.

SOCRATES: [Let] us make in each [person's mind] a sort of aviary of all kinds of birds; some in flocks separate from the others, some in small groups, and other flying about singly here and there among all the rest.

THEAETETUS: All right, let us suppose it made. What then?

SOCRATES: Then we must say that when we are children this receptacle is empty; and by the birds we must understand pieces of knowledge. When anyone takes possession of a piece of knowledge and shuts it up in the pen, we should say that he has learned or has found out the thing of which this is the knowledge; and knowing, we should say, is this.

THEAETETUS: That's given, then.

SOCRATES: Now think: when he hunts again for any one of the pieces of knowledge that he chooses, and takes it and "has" it, then lets it go again, what words are appropriate here? The same as before, when he took possession of the knowledge, or different ones?—You will see my point more clearly in this way. There is an art you call arithmetic, isn't there?

THEAETETUS: Yes.

SOCRATES: Now I want you to think of this as a hunt for pieces of knowledge concerning everything odd and even.

THEAETETUS: All right, I will.

SOCRATES: It is by virtue of this art, I suppose, that a man both has under his control pieces of knowledge concerning numbers, and also hands them over to others?

THEAETETUS: Yes.

SOCRATES: And we call it "teaching" when a man hands them over to others, and "learning" when he gets them handed over to him; and when he "has" them through possessing them in this aviary of ours, we call that "knowing."

THEAETETUS: Yes, certainly.

SOCRATES: Now you must give your attention to what is coming next. It must surely be true that a man who has completely mastered arithmetic knows all numbers? Because there are pieces of knowledge covering all numbers in his [mind.]

THEAETETUS: Of course.

SOCRATES: And a man so trained may proceed to do some counting, either counting to himself the numbers themselves, or counting something else, one of the external things which have number?

THEAETETUS: Yes, surely.

SOCRATES: And counting we shall take to be simply a matter of considering how large a number actually is?

THEAETETUS: Yes.

SOCRATES: Then it looks as if this man were considering something which he knows as if he did not know it (for we have granted that he knows all numbers). I've no doubt you've had such puzzles put to you.

THEAETETUS: I have, yes.

SOCRATES: Then using our image of possessing and hunting for the pigeons, we shall say that there are two phases of hunting; one before you have possession in order to get possession, and another when you already possess in order to catch and have in your hands what you previously acquired. And in this way even with things you learned and got the knowledge of long ago and have known ever since, it is possible to learn them—these same things—all over again. You can take up again and "have" that knowledge of each of them which you acquired long ago but had not ready to hand in your thought, can't you?

THEAETETUS: True.[3]

in more than 1,600 communities across the United States. The larger goal of these two geniuses—and staunch book lovers—was to stimulate thinking in the local community—and among humanity. These examples illustrate that a library without values is just a building. What makes it a library are the values it expresses. These values can be passed along from director to director and from generation to generation.

NOTES

1. Martin Zwilling, "Learn to 'Do the Right Thing' for your Startup," *Forbes.com*, May 17, 2011, http://onforb.es/MsVy4W.
2. Plato, *Plato: Complete Works*, ed. John M. Cooper (Indianapolis, IN: Hackett, 1997), 219–20.
3. Plato, *Plato: Complete Works*, 218–20.

Three

TAKING INTELLIGENT RISKS

Life is either a daring adventure or nothing at all.

HELEN KELLER

Are you willing to see the forest—that is, the overarching purpose of the library as enlightening humanity—and not just the trees, such as collections, technology, programs, data, and services? Are you willing to take a risk by focusing on individual and community needs—and not just your personal expectations? A would-be entrepreneur takes risks by coming to the library to seek information to learn how to start up a small business. A family takes risks by coming to the library's robotics program with the hope to learn and have fun together. A teen takes risks by asking a library staffer to recommend a book to read hoping it'll fulfill his or her yearning to be engaged in something worthwhile.

The real steps forward within the library profession—like in any aspect of society, such as education, business, or government—are taken by risk-takers. Can you strengthen your risk muscle? How? A starting point to build risk skills is to ask yourself—and ponder—a series of questions, right questions. What is a "right" question? First, a wrong question is one such as, why do giraffes have eight legs? Since giraffes have four legs, it's not a good question because the answer can never be right. It's not productive to ask a question such as, do goodwill and peace exist, but instead ask how we can tap goodwill and peace within ourselves to help the library enrich the community. A right question is one with a right answer. Other examples: How well do you tolerate uncertainty? Do you look forward to a constant flux of information in order to sort it out quickly and capture the best data? Are you in tune with an intelligent instinct of how to proceed when taking a risk? Can you look at mistakes and failures as opportunities to celebrate learning? Can you spot a "good risk" when you see one?

Humanity has grown the most through regular redefinitions of society, including both success and scandal. For example, we take risks that people will be forthright in fulfilling their responsibilities, will treat others as they would like to be treated, and will devote their best skills and talents to each endeavor. Without taking a risk to redefine and update ourselves, our organizations, and our communities, we miss excellent opportunities to expand our capacity to cope with setbacks, to derive contentment from our work, to experience serenity, and to strive for the highest level of achievement. *Librarians are far more experienced in intelligent risk-taking than we might realize.* Although they may seem insignificant, our daily decisions, interactions, and commitments to serve our patrons are at the heart of invigorating and redefining our communities. In everyday library transactions, one-on-one discussions, and engagement activities—keeping in mind the broader aim to inspire human growth—librarians are helping people transform their lives. It is through the mundane that we reach higher levels of personal triumph and community accomplishment.

Library administrators and staffers can strengthen their risk muscles by developing a high level of readiness for risk-taking. A library that stays in touch with its community by responding to its challenges will help move the community forward. It doesn't matter what a town, neighborhood, or city is facing—whether it is economic, cultural, educational, health, or safety issues—these challenges can be turned into opportunities for learning, growing, and thriving. Let's drive this point home further: success is often the result of our ability to take risks. *For librarians, the more we can support our community to take risks—educators, public officials, parents, businesspeople, and anyone connecting to library service—the more a community is ready to grow.*

Life is filled with risks. The way we assess a risk helps determine whether taking that risk will be a foolish or smart move. Figuring out how to assess each risk is a valuable tool—and will strengthen your ability to take intelligent risks. Ask yourself: how can you tell whether a risk is short-sighted or intelligent? Let's explore how! The Proto-Indo-European origin of the word "risk" means "to leap, climb," in other words, to overcome obstacles that seem to be in the way. When a library director prepares a grant application to fund a large makerspace, she may be uncertain of the outcome but she knows that even if the project is not funded, she and other staff will be able to use the research data for future projects. The seeming obstacle—thinking that it's not worth the time to write a grant because we may not be awarded funding—is overcome. When library administrators conduct a study to determine whether the library's business center is impacting the growth of entrepreneurship in the community, the process of implementing the study, no matter what the outcome, is a solid investment in time to gain information in order to improve service.

When a young mother searches the Internet for an answer to a health question for her baby, she is taking a leap of faith that she will find something helpful among the 35 million "hits." How can libraries help her to discern what may be harmful or helpful for her specific situation?

An exemplary risk-taker from Victorian England was the Irish-born writer Oscar Wilde. He used his wit and writing skills to shake the literary world out of its complacency with great insight, humor, and inspiration. Although his career and life ended in scandal, his outstanding works of poetry, plays, short stories, and a novel helped people to unlearn old habits and inspired them to embrace new ways of thinking.

You may be familiar with the play *The Importance of Being Earnest* or the novel *The Picture of Dorian Gray* by Wilde. Have you read any of his poems or short stories, such as "The Nightingale and the Rose" or "The Happy Prince"? In the 1887 short story "The Model Millionaire: A Note of Admiration," Hughie Erskine, a young man—although poor in materialistic terms—is generous in heart and mind. Hughie thoughtfully expresses his generosity one day by giving the largest coin in his pocket to someone who needs it more than he does. Although he ponders whether his money will be squandered, he is willing to take the risk. Hughie demonstrates the value of investing in life itself—which often has unexpected positive outcomes.

IN QUEST OF DISCOVERIES

By sharing our talents, skills, goodwill, and generosity, we are taking an intelligent risk. By developing curiosity, expanding our ability to live with uncertainty, and by learning to unlearn, we are strengthening—and flexing—our risk muscle. By discovering fresh perspectives on the potential of our organization and community, we increase the likelihood of pursuing intelligent risks. By examining what needs to be unlearned, we increase our risk-readiness skills. How can we unlearn habits that produce poor results? The "If I get angry, I'll get my way" syndrome may work in the short term, but will it improve morale in the long run? Is a large dose of worry the only fail-safe ingredient to solve a problem? Many of today's librarians are on the cutting edge of supporting and coaching breakthroughs in their own, their coworkers', and their customers' lifelong learning, and thus invigorating the growth of humanity.

What happens if a perceived intelligent risk fails or ends up—gasp— as a scandal? Let's examine the phenomenon of scandal, which relates to Plato's question of what's true and what's false. The truth behind many "scandals"—ancient or modern—often hides a deeper reality. Socrates was scandalized—and put to death—for supposedly corrupting the minds of youths by asking questions to encourage them to think for themselves. The real scandal was the deception of the Athenian people by their leaders; that is, by paying too much attention to their leaders, the Athenian people were misled into executing Socrates. The affair of the diamond necklace in 1771 was based on false accusations against Queen Marie Antoinette, Count Cagliostro, and other members of the court, yet it was a key factor in bringing down the French monarchy.

What happens if a perceived intelligent risk ends up not as scandal, but as a failure? The Old English word "fail" means to "be unsuccessful in accomplishing a purpose" and to "come to an end." In pondering these definitions, a failure can be seen in a broader context as an opportunity to accomplish the library's purpose in a new way. *It is a new beginning.* Edward de Bono says, "One does not mind being wrong on the way to a solution because it may be necessary to go through a wrong area in order to get to a position from which the correct path is visible."[1] Some people may experience a mistake or failure as a setback, a misadventure, or worse—as a defeat. Intelligent risk-takers learn to look at the same situation and use it as a time for reexamination and a celebration of learning and growth.

Exploration can turn some failures into unexpected successes. For example, in the 1920s, while struggling to solve a customer's need for the waterproof covering of insulation batts or precut panels for railroad refrigerator cars, the 3M engineer Richard Drew ended up developing "Scotch" tape. The product was a failure in terms of not fulfilling the original problem or need of the railroad industry, but it gave the world a practical—and tremendously successful and useful—household and office commodity. "Farmers found it handy for patching cracked turkey eggs. Homeowners used it to repair toys and torn book pages. New uses continue to be discovered—and product sales continue to grow—up to the present day."[2]

Librarians who go to their community in quest of discoveries will find unlimited human potential—no matter what the community's composition. Finding—and cultivating—human potential can seem a little vague. What does it mean, after all? The goal is to reveal what Plato called "the good" in others. Benjamin Franklin described being your best in order to "work for the common good." Abraham Lincoln stated, "Whatever you are, be a good one." Developing the habit to think things through will help us learn skills, make wise decisions, and expand opportunities. Let's celebrate all that's good in the community—and connect it to the library. Community collaboration, connecting with individuals, families, and businesses, and focusing on the potential of those in our neighborhood will help librarians develop—and master—intelligent risk-taking.

Libraries are investing in emerging technologies and creating incubator work groups to investigate what may or may not work. "We take risks by experimenting with new technologies. Our applied technologies team asks: How might our customers benefit? Who in the community needs to be involved? Is this a fad or does it have staying power? What should we invest in? What has the best chance of success?" says Bob Kuntz, director of operations and innovation at the Carroll County (MD) Public Library.

"It's pretty cool to imagine how many people will try virtual reality for the very first time—and have that 'wow' moment—in their local libraries," says the Oculus education program manager Cindy Ball. "We hope early access will cause many people to feel excited and empowered to move beyond just experiencing virtual reality and open their minds to the possibility of one day joining the industry."[3]

"We wanted to apply several new ideas about the potential of library space into what became Library 21c, a branch of the Pikes Peak Library District," explains Paula Miller, the current director of the Baltimore County (MD) Public Library. As the former director at Pikes Peak, Miller oversaw the risky renovation of the old tech giant MCI's national headquarters building and the transformation of its 120,000 square feet into a library where the "c" in Library 21c stands not only for "century" but also for *change, connections, create,* and *community.* The previous space, in comparison, served residents in a 7,500-square-foot storefront library branch.

A group of local filmmakers were auditioning for a new project one spring Saturday afternoon lauding Library 21c's Center for Public Media—which

FIGURE 3.1

Virtual reality hands-on
opportunities at the library.

Photo: Courtesy of Carroll County (MD)
Public Library

is designed to help future filmmakers, video producers, musicians, and others produce their own high-quality videos. "Ralph Giordano, a local director, started the Peak Film Forum here at the library four years ago with six people showing up for that first meeting. We now have hundreds of people attending our meetings, networking, and producing wonderful projects," says Eliot Johnson, who is in film and video production.

As one library patron posted on the library's website, "Gosh, this place rules. Be prepared to have your idea of a library blown out of the water!!"[4] Besides offering books and the public media center, Library 21c features an array of modern facilities such as a creative computer commons area, a business center, a terraced open space under skylights, a video-gaming area, an e-lab, a separate teen space, a huge children's area, a café, a 400-seat community meeting room and theater, a career assistance center, and a variety of makerspaces. A wide range of classes, programs, services, and roving librarians help the community explore personal interests—and take risks.

Risks are seldom this spectacular. John Spears, the current Pikes Peak (CO) Library director and president (2016–17) of the Library Leadership & Management Association, says, "People can go to Library 21c and use its recording studio and record an album. However, on our library's website, you can check out local music you're not going to find at a record store or on iTunes. That's an easier role that many libraries—no matter what their size of budget, staff, or space—could play: linking to the local music scene within their own community. Another focus for any library is seeing what the issues are in each community and letting the library be a neutral public space to discuss them. During the presidential election year, there were a lot of issues people wanted to talk about. People are very passionate about these issues, but increasingly, people are living in their own echo chambers. The library can give the community breathing room to have those discussions and hopefully talk with others who don't necessarily think the way that they do."

Another example of risk-taking in action is the Baltimore County (BCPL) Public Library's Storyville playscapes, which are housed in two branches and target children from birth to age five, along with their parents and caregivers. Before library play-and-learn centers became more popular across the country, Storyville at the Rosedale branch of the BCPL was opened in 2007 as a large, separate play space—an entire wing in the building—and offered a whimsical combination of museum, early childhood center, and children's library.

A parent visiting Storyville says, "We come every week. You can see in every center that learning is the goal. After coming here, my child asks me to help sort socks and tell me about the colors. She also asked about different types of food at the grocery store."[5] Although most libraries cannot afford a million-dollar renovation to transform a wing of a library into a large play-scape, any library can create a high-quality play-and-learn spot with very little money, space, or materials.

Library administrators across the country are taking the chance that library boards, staff, and community members will support patrons engaged in joyful—and audible—learning inside their buildings. "The design and

FIGURE 3.2

The United States Air Force Academy Concert Band performs a concert in the atrium of the Pikes Peak Library District's Library 21c.

Photo: Courtesy of Pikes Peak (CO) Library District's Library 21c

FIGURE 3.3

Storyville Rosedale, Baltimore County Public Library, Maryland.

Photo: Courtesy of Baltimore County (MD) Public Library

FIGURE 3.4

Inside Storyville Store, Baltimore County Public Library, Maryland.

Photo: Courtesy of Baltimore County (MD) Public Library

FIGURE 3.5

Inside Storyville House, Baltimore County Public Library, Maryland.

Photo: Courtesy of Baltimore County (MD) Public Library

implementation of playscapes, 'makerspaces,' and 'tech labs' are transforming public libraries and invigorating communities," says Carrie Sanders, youth services coordinator at the Maryland State Library. Although these innovative spaces—large, medium, or small—are often popular and successful with people of all ages, they can be "risky" because they are changing the traditional library environment. Communities value the expanded scope of library service that offers discovery learning through play, tinkering, and exploration. At the same time, how can a library offer a balance of playful discovery areas alongside quiet nooks and crannies, study areas, and spots for contemplation and reflection?

Whether changing the environment or offering new technology options and digital media mentoring, libraries should learn to take intelligent risks and recognize "failures"—as Richard Drew, the unintentional inventor of Scotch tape, did—as new opportunities. Risk-taking is mostly accomplished by librarians tending to the small details of meeting the needs of customers. You don't need unlimited funding to stimulate new thinking through discussion programs, setting up relationships with businesses, or offering experiential learning activities during the summer. Everyday risk-taking could distinguish a library in the community—and endear it to the people it serves for years to come. By nurturing a daily readiness for risk-taking—by flexing their risk muscles—librarians are embracing a journey of discovery, an adventure of daring, and a mindset to spark curiosity in order to help communities meet their challenges and flourish.

NOTES

1. Edward de Bono, *Lateral Thinking: Creativity Step by Step* (1970; New York: Harper Perennial, 2015), 232.
2. The Great Idea Finder, www.ideafinder.com/history/inventions/cellophanetape.htm.
3. *Oculus* blog, June 7, 2017, https://www.oculus.com/blog/oculus-education-pilot-kicks -off-in-90-california-libraries/.
4. Yelp, https://www.yelp.com/biz/library-21c-colorado-springs.
5. Dorothy Stoltz, Marisa Conner, and James Bradberry, *The Power of Play: Designing Early Learning Spaces* (Chicago: American Library Association, 2015), 161.

PART II

TREASURE THOSE YOU SERVE . . . SO THEY WILL SERVE YOU

Four

THE GOLDEN RULE

Trust men and they will be true to you; treat them greatly,
and they will show themselves great.

RALPH WALDO EMERSON

Everyone has an opinion about the Golden Rule, but many of us don't understand it. If you think it is an old-fashioned sentiment, a fanciful notion, or just a churchly nicety, join us for a journey to upgrade our insight into this timeless concept of community goodwill and make it practical for everyday library business. Are you ready to think this through? If so, read on!

Library administrators who thrive treasure staff members who not only know how to take intelligent risks, but also know how to value and deliver excellent customer service. By examining what's working, what's not working, and what can be done differently in order to be more effective—on a regular basis—we can identify emerging strategies and bring fresh insights and new enthusiasm into the library profession.

We value listening to people in the community as a way to understand what the library can do to create better services. "We are upping the ante and finding new ways to conduct the traditional library reference interview. Through a thoughtful and dedicated approach, we are increasingly touching customers at their point of need," says Wesley Wilson, director of the Maryland State Library Resource Center.

Exceptional customer service is a leading priority. Top-notch service has embraced the saying that "the customer is always right"—or variations promoted since the early twentieth century: "the customer is never wrong," "give the lady what she wants," "if a diner complains about a dish or the wine, immediately remove it and replace it, no questions asked," or "the customer is king." The maxim was revised—due to foolish television ads—to become: "the customer is not a moron," "the customer is not an idiot; "she's your wife, so stop laughing," "the customer is you," or "if we want to understand our customers, we're going to have to understand them extremely well." These service mottos come from pioneering and successful business and marketing people such as Henry Gordon Selfridge (retail), Cezar Ritz (hotel), Marshall Field (retail), David Ogilvy (advertising), Austin McGhie (marketing), and James Leibert (business).

Of course, this old adage—the customer is always right—may not apply in all situations, or does it? If we think it through in each situation, we will always focus on what is needed to "make the customer *right*"—to create optimal customer service. Although some people look for opportunities to steal library items or find ways to circumvent library rules, can we apply creative solutions to address these situations so the majority of patrons do not lose out? When other people behave badly or in some way adversely affect a library learning environment, employee time, or resources, can library staffers handle these circumstances with patience and poise while finding community solutions? Let's explore how to harness the best in library and customer service—without dishonest, troubled, or other individuals taking undue advantage of the library.

THE CUSTOMER ALWAYS WINS

When a customer offers feedback that we don't necessarily enjoy hearing or it seems to be wrong, he or she is "right" in that we need to listen and learn. On the one hand, we can't permit a library patron to make policy, but on the other hand, he or she can help define service that is best suited for the community—and may end up helping to change an out-of-date policy or procedure. For example, a library may traditionally offer informational—non-advocacy— programs about religious or spiritual practices that are not representative of the majority of the community as a way to teach about different religions or cultures. However, can library staff members embrace a request from a library patron asking for an informational and discussion program about the dominant belief in the community— whatever that might be—and do so without becoming annoyed, offended, or provoked? A library may think it is celebrating different viewpoints in its collection by offering a few token best sellers about a particular issue or by a particular author, but miss the opportunity to fully explore the community's interest in one side or the other.

Can those of us working in libraries hone the skills of an emerging practice: it's not the details of right and wrong in a customer service situation that matter as much as it is the larger perspective that the person in front of you—in person, on the phone, or online—is a dissatisfied customer. A library patron may not know how a library works. Patrons see rules and policies as limitations and restrictions that are holding them back from accomplishing a task, exploring a new idea, or connecting to valuable information. If they feel hurt by the experience, then they are hurt for all intents and purposes. The goal is not to point out that a patron is "wrong," but to solve each situation as quickly and amiably as possible.

Let's examine the value of sincerity in customer service. Too many times library staffers—or those in retail and other businesses—pay only lip service to customers who are complaining or expressing a concern. It doesn't matter whether the concern is legitimate or not. If we are treating library patrons superficially, then that's what we'll receive in return. A patron may leave the library thinking, "I've just been conned by the librarian." Insincerity can be spotted a mile away. However, the genuine expression of sincerity really counts. If we are sincere to our customers, then they will be sincere to us—and will want to support the library. By launching into excellent customer service with the approach "Let me do whatever I can to make it right," librarians will take away any sense of hurt or confusion. For some library staffers, this technique may be new—and will require practice. However, the results will be well worth it. This approach strengthens our ability to persuade our customers to continue using—and supporting—the library.

"Consequences of our acts are eternal?" asks Blawkins, a character at the beginning of the 1887 short story "The Track of a Lie" by Rudyard Kipling. A journalist and his friend discuss a piece of useless misinformation which, when the former prints it in his newspaper, turns out to be what Kipling coined "a liftable stick," an eye-catching quotation, that is repeated by newspapers all round the world. This tale goes on to demonstrate how a short passage about a superstition can first appear somewhere—in this case, in a local newspaper in southern India—and end up a year later as "truth" all around the world. Of course, today, we have the Internet and many forms of online communication that do the same thing—news heard 'round the world—but with immediate impact.

The current social media avenue gives library patrons an instantaneous pathway to praise or complain about a storytime, a book in the collection, or anything else about the library—and therefore may influence hundreds or thousands of people in your community. Alex Knapp, the *Forbes* editor of social media, says:

> Your philosophy needs to boil down to just one principle: be a decent human being. Or, to paraphrase several philosophers, *do unto your customers as you want to be treated when you're a customer*. This principle is all you need when designing your customer service policies and procedures. If you find that your customers are complaining about how you provide customer service, start putting yourself in their shoes.[1]

We may need to unlearn what we think we know about the Golden Rule. It is not the equivalent of sport mottos—"tackle them hard because they are going to tackle us hard," or "break their bones before they break our bones."

The Golden Rule—or the ethic of reciprocity—can be found throughout history in all major cultures, philosophies, and religions. Why should librarians strive to be "decent human beings" and care about how we treat people? If libraries are not providing exceptional customer service and do not "treasure" the people we serve, then what do we expect the public to do, but discontinue funding? That's what this book is about. It is deadly for libraries to take public support for granted.

The ethic of reciprocity is not only a successful business practice, as Knapp explains, but it is a good practice in all aspects of life. It is not only a helpful proverb for the religious-minded, but is a guideline for anyone, anytime and anywhere, to express a common-sense approach to achieve a measure of success in life.

On a practical level, our goal is to serve people and fulfill community needs. What better way to provide services, activities, and resources than in a manner that guarantees—or nearly so—the reciprocity of support to keep the library open. Treasuring those we serve in order for them to support library service is expedient, pragmatic, and doable.

Although applying the Golden Rule—or this golden law of life—does not in any way encourage a library staffer to join a religion or master Shakespeare or take a philosophy class, it does require learning to express ourselves using cheerfulness, tolerance, courage, and self-control. By using gentle thoughts towards others—even when they are nasty—we enable ourselves to more easily serve people. By applying compassion toward ourselves and others on a regular basis—especially when mistakes are made—we become more patient.

This core value—treating others as you would like to be treated—is the essence of brotherhood, human rights, and the enlightenment of humanity. It—and related virtues—can be found in the texts of many great thinkers, education theory, and popular literature. Let's explore the common thread of the Golden Rule woven throughout history, culture, and the world:

It does not seem to be just to treat anyone badly,
not even an enemy.

—Plato, *The Republic*

The Golden Rule is of no use to you whatsoever unless you realize
that it's your move!

—*School Leadership from A to Z: Practical Lessons from Successful Schools and Businesses*
(2003) by Robert D. Ramsey

Love your neighbor as yourself.

—Moses, Leviticus 19:18

If you are an entrepreneur planning to start your own company,
I can't think of a better place to begin than by operating your
business by the Golden Rule. Make this a high priority; never make
a decision that contradicts the Golden Rule.

—Mary Kay Ash, American businesswoman and founder of Mary Kay Cosmetics, Inc.

What you do not wish upon yourself, extend not to others.

—Confucius

My mother and father would say, "If people would only live by the
Golden Rule, there wouldn't be the problems that there are."
In other words, "treat people the way you want to be treated."
If somebody mistreats you, two wrongs won't make a right.

—Monte Irvin, baseball player

A fool thinks himself to be wise,
but a wise man knows himself to be a fool.

—William Shakespeare, *As You Like It*

Mrs. Do-As-You-Would-Be-Done-By and
Mrs. Be-Done-By-As-You-Did

—characters in *The Water Babies* (1863) by Charles Kingsley

What is hateful to you, do not to your fellow man.

—Hillel the Elder

Do unto others as you would have them do unto you.

—Jesus, Luke 6:31, Luke 10:27, Matthew 7:12

Do unto all men as you would wish to have done unto you.

—Muhammad, *Abu Dawud*

Life is by nature good and desirable . . . and if as the virtuous
man is to himself, he is to his friend also (for his friend is another
self):—if all this be true, as his own being is desirable for each man,
so, or almost so, is that of his friend.

—Aristotle, *Nicomachean Ethics*

With malice toward none, with charity for all.

—Abraham Lincoln, Second Inaugural Address

While inspiring strategic plans and uplifting customer-service training play important functions in weaving an exceptional customer service tapestry, we need even more urgently to be intelligent and kind staffers who are skillful and dedicated at treating others the way they want to be treated. If a patron is a creative, energetic tech entrepreneur in search of networking, connect him with the library's technology activities, volunteer coordinator, and the local tech council. If a patron is a drug addict who has overdosed, administer Narcan and apply CPR until the ambulance arrives. If a patron is a new mother excited about her infant son's first storytime, encourage and mentor her to use the library as a resource for early childhood information, for books and toys, for socializing, and for sparking her curiosity about becoming the best parent she can be.

Reciprocity between a library serving the community and the community paying for a library seems obvious, but this is not always the case. The more libraries focus on meeting community needs and offering exceptional service, the more public and private funds will support the library. The goal

FIGURE 4.1

Patrons enjoying an adaptation of *Twelfth Night* as told from the perspective of Malvolio. In 2016 the Cleveland Public Library (CPL) had year-round programming that included performances, screenings, and discussions celebrating the 400th anniversary of Shakespeare's death. Thanks to the Folger Shakespeare Library in Washington, DC, the CPL was the only institution in Ohio to showcase the Shakespeare First Folio during its 2016 tour.

Photo: Courtesy of Cleveland Public Library

is to establish a genuine relationship between the library and the people it deems to serve. For example, "by talking with people all over the city and in many walks of life," says Felton Thomas, director of the Cleveland (OH) Public Library and president (2016–17) of the Public Library Association, "we've learned how library tutoring and a free meal can support a single mom struggling to help her children succeed in school. We've learned about the generosity of wealthy Clevelanders engaged in philanthropic projects to do good in the community."

A Trader Joe's grocery store in Pennsylvania stepped up to give excellent—perhaps what some might describe as shocking or startling—customer service when an 89-year-old man became homebound during a snowstorm around the holidays. After his daughter called several grocers in the area to no avail, she asked Trader Joe's if they would deliver. The employee responded that they would do so in this instance. He not only delivered the order—within thirty minutes—but didn't charge the family for the food or delivery and wished them a Merry Christmas.[2]

Let's emulate Trader Joe's outstanding customer service. Let's echo the great thinkers by striving to live the Golden Rule. As we serve people by using the golden law of reciprocity, we establish proper priorities of library service based on individual community needs. We enhance opportunities for support from those we serve. And we discover how to treat everyone in our community "greatly" and allow them to show themselves great!

NOTES

1. Alex Knapp, "The Golden Rule of Customer Service," *Forbes.com*, July 2, 2012, www.forbes.com/sites/alexknapp/2012/07/02/the-golden-rule-of-customer-service/#5ca156363d56.

2. Glenn Stansberry, "10 Examples of Shockingly Excellent Customer Service," *American Express Open Forum.com*, May 4, 2010, https://www.americanexpress.com/us/small-business/openforum/articles/10-examples-of-shockingly-excellent-customer-service-1/.

Five

RESPECT AND GOODWILL

The best thing to give to your enemy is forgiveness; to an opponent,
tolerance; to a friend, your heart; to your child, a good example;
to a father, deference; to your mother, conduct that will make her
proud of you; to yourself, respect; to all men, charity.

BENJAMIN FRANKLIN

How can library administrators and staffers cope with people who disagree with them, push their buttons, or seem antithetical to their beliefs? Many librarians, but not everyone, are able to maintain political and religious neutrality. However, is it genuine neutrality? Or is it just a prejudice in disguise? How do we encourage those of us in the library field to think through the concepts of respect and community goodwill—thoroughly and completely—and express them?

Community goodwill can be defined as a force to do "good" and build a constructive bond with those we serve. It is tied to the purpose of the library—the enlightenment of humanity. Respect is in essence the same as goodwill but is expressed as a mental habit. For example, do most of us working in libraries—automatically and instinctively—treat everyone using the library with respect: the drug addict, the elected official from the "other" party, the gay teacher, the Spanish-speaking family, or the local millionaire? Or do we cringe inside? We may put on a good show by camouflaging our discomfort, but we may silently convey or broadcast an element of disappointment or disapproval.

The library is one of many elements that make up a community, from individuals and families to businesses and organizations. A community needs every element, every viewpoint, and every person striving to be their best; it cannot thrive without all parts working together. The library can play a key role in the success of a community, especially in setting a tone for how we treat each other as we deliver services and programs.

Respect and goodwill are intangible elements, but they are not frivolous, imponderable, or illusory. The library can create an atmosphere and aura of respect and goodwill. However, it can only do so if those working in the library are willing to actively enact policy. Otherwise, library staffers can sabotage respect and goodwill. For example, do they speak disrespectfully about community leaders or other individuals or groups on library time with colleagues and patrons? Is this type of behavior left unchecked by supervisors? Do supervisors indulge in these types of conversations too? When it comes to politics, religion, and social issues, the library that thrives expresses no opinion and maintains a neutral stance.

Besides promoting a neutral stance on hot topics, a library can instill respect and goodwill in other practical and pragmatic ways. Internally, a library organization can develop core values and expectations that govern how staff work together and treat each other. Externally, it can design customer service policies and expectations that govern how staff members act toward the community. We can set the tone for how to respect every member and element of the community—no matter what a person's reputation, income, politics, religion, lifestyle, or education.

Do you need to know why some people avoid making eye contact when they interact with you at the service desk? No! Does it matter whether it is because the person's culture views direct eye contact as hostile and rude, or because he is shy, or because he is partially blind, or because he is affected by a form of autism? Again, no! What matters is meeting the person where he is and providing exceptional customer service.

One tool—of many organizational tools that can assist libraries in their work to invigorate themselves and their communities—is the concept of the learning organization. Connecting to a larger purpose and to other people is a foundational human desire. Peter Senge, the creator of "learning organizations" in the business world, developed techniques to help employees think things through, strive to understand the whole organization, and use the tool of shared aspiration to produce worthy results. "The spirit of connection is undermined whenever we lose respect for one another or for each other's views. We then split into insiders and outsiders. This connection, and the effectiveness of a shared vision, grows whenever mutual respect is obvious," says Senge.[1]

If a community partner using a library meeting room goes to the service desk asking for copies and hears this response: "I need to get approval," in that instant, the library is conveying a lack of respect. The staffer returns from the back room to say: "The supervisors are discussing it. Someone will come out and let you know the decision." A supervisor appears after several minutes saying: "I'm not sure if I can make your copies. How many do you need? I've got to pay for the paper." Zap! That's another flash of disrespect. The community partner is in danger of misinterpreting the concern of the supervisor to cover her actions as not caring about the request. It transmits the idea that "my job is more important than your request."

A supervisor or staffer covering her actions focuses her attention on deniability and contradicts her ability to serve the public. How can this contradiction be resolved? It is necessary to push authority out to front-line supervisors and staff members. It is important to train them well to think things through and make wise decisions. If someone on the service desk makes a decision that a manager or director disagrees with, then the helpful response of the latter is: "I'm glad you were comfortable using authority because you respected the patron. That's important. With this kind of request in future, do it this way, and not that way."

Over the years, the Public Library Association and many state and local libraries, including ones in Arizona, Idaho, Illinois, Maryland, and Wyoming, have adopted learning organizational concepts. "An organization, through its personnel policies, training programs, and one-on-one mentoring efforts, develops the discipline of personal mastery among its employees," says Betsy Bernfeld, author and former director of the Teton County (WY) Library. Mastering respect for yourself and other people creates goodwill toward all—and creates opportunities for a library to thrive. Bernfeld continues, "A library is not just a storehouse of information. It is not a reflection of a librarian's interests. It should be a vibrant participant in the life of the community and be constantly looking to the community for its mission and direction."[2]

Senge weaves respect and goodwill throughout the five learning organizational principles—systems thinking, personal mastery, mental models, building shared vision, and team learning. These principles were embedded in the Carroll County Public Library's culture in the 1990s. Although that library doesn't necessarily use the terminology today, the practices are evident. The energy of respect and goodwill has been magnified over the years, both internally and externally. One small example of its long-term impact is how the library consistently increases its ability to collaborate with public schools, private schools, and homeschool students. A bond of mutual respect and goodwill has built effective relationships between the library and these school organizations, despite changes in personnel. In recent years, a reading initiative for elementary and middle school students, "Battle of the Books," began with 2 contests, 15 teams, and 180 students in one library branch. Within six years, the popular reading initiative expanded across the county to all six branches, featuring 9 contests with 235 teams and over 1,500 participants.

Successfully managing a period of great challenge and problem-solving can result in strengthening mutual respect within a group. One way to promote goodwill within a group is to acknowledge and celebrate each other's contributions. Paula Singer, an author and organizational development consultant, says, "Taking time for acknowledgement, recognition and celebration of successes is [key to an organization's growth], and often the most inexpensive, personal gestures can make the biggest difference."[3]

FIGURE 5.1

Collaborative activities can foster a bond of mutual respect between schools and libraries. A "Battle of the Books" reading contest planned and implemented by the Carroll County Public Library and local schools reflects the trust and goodwill to take risks together.

Photo: Courtesy of Carroll County Public Library

An excellent thinking technique—to help increase our understanding of the value of respect and goodwill in our work in libraries—is Socrates's "lead an examined life" approach.

LEADING AN EXAMINED LIFE WITH SOCRATES

Socrates encouraged his students to lead an examined life. By reading, pondering, and digesting Socrates, we can learn about the value of regularly examining or reflecting on the results of our thoughts, decisions, and actions. Recurring themes from Socrates and other Greek philosophers, such as Aristotle, Plato, and Parmenides, help us strive for the ideal in life—slowly cultivating a broad understanding of concepts like respect and goodwill and downloading them into everyday life. Let's translate this approach from an example of the Socratic thinking method and pose a few practical questions for the librarian.

In book II of Plato's *The Republic*, a conversation—among Socrates, Adeimantus, and Plato's brother, Glaucon—reveals the value of thoughtful examination and can be applied to understanding concepts such as respect and goodwill. Socrates discusses how people need each other to support life. Each individual plays a role and contributes to society. When individuals learn to bring out the best in themselves and in each other, the community can thrive.

> *Socrates*: Where are we to find a character that is both gentle and high-spirited at the same time? After all, a gentle nature is the opposite of a spirited one.
>
> *Glaucon*: Apparently.
>
> *Socrates*: If someone lacks either gentleness [respect for him or herself and for others] or spirit [courage and vitality], he can't be a good [person]. Yet it seems impossible to combine them . . . [The love of learning can bring out the best in oneself. It can help each person cultivate respect, courage, and goodwill.] Surely the love of learning [the right things] is the same thing as philosophy or the love of wisdom.
>
> *Glaucon*: It is.

Socrates: Then, may we confidently assume . . . that if he is to be gentle [and respectful] toward his own and those he knows, he must be a lover of learning and wisdom?

Glaucon: Absolutely.[4]

Socrates thought through the concept that each individual can strive to be both gentle and spirited. In this way, the community benefits. By asking right questions—ones that lead to the results you want—library administrators and staffers can examine how they practice respect and goodwill and thus serve as a model for the community.

Let's examine our core values—and build a habit of respect and goodwill toward ourselves and others. Let's celebrate! "Too frequently, good cheer, friendliness, and goodwill are considered signs of weakness," say Robert Leichtman and Carl Japikse.[5] The secret is to achieve a balance between passive and active qualities and to discern and express them intelligently.

FIGURE 5.2

The participants of "Crochet It!: A Creative Community Project" learn to crochet circles to be installed on two trees on the Middle Country (NY) Public Library's property. "Crochet It!" is a community-focused tree-wrapping project that involves the independent creation of thousands of colorful crocheted circles. This project will culminate in two unique art installations at the library to be enjoyed by all for years to come. Crocheting and other hands-on activities cultivate a tone of helpfulness and celebration.

Photo: Courtesy of Middle Country (NY) Public Library

For example, we can learn the difference between optimism and naiveté and between helpfulness and foolishness. We can figure out how to harmonize qualities, such as optimism and helpfulness, in order to communicate goodwill.

> With a nod to Otis Redding and Aretha Franklin:
> A little respect (just a little bit)
> R-E-S-P-E-C-T
> Find it @ the library
> R-E-S-P-E-C-T
> Take care, TCB

David K. Williams, author and CEO of Fishbowl Inventory, condemns a lack of respect as something that harms company employees or customers. He makes respect a "keystone" for doing business and says, "If employees say something rude or dishonest, or fail to do something they committed to do, they can't just say, 'I'm sorry.' Sorry is a start; but to make a genuine difference, you must make changes, which would mean a consistent positive effort and possibly even restitution and reparation."[6] Fishbowl doesn't advocate that their employees wallow in guilt, but seek the right balance to make amends beyond a superficial apology.

Here are a few questions to help you examine your daily work in the course of building the habit of respect and goodwill toward all:

FIGURE 5.3

Aretha Franklin sings "My Country 'Tis of Thee'" at the U.S. Capitol during the 56th presidential inauguration in Washington, DC, on January 20, 2009.

Photo: Cecilio Ricardo, U.S. Air Force

- How can you weave the qualities of optimism and helpfulness into library service?
- How can you use goodwill to improve your programs, services, and collections?
- Can you stay focused on determining how to make your community proud, and not become sidetracked by bringing personal causes to work?
- How do you build a mental habit of respect for yourself, your colleagues, and all elements of the community?

NOTES

1. Peter M. Senge, *The Fifth Discipline: The Art & Practice of the Learning Organization* (New York: Doubleday Business, 1990).
2. Betsy A. Bernfeld, "Developing a Team Management Structure in a Public Library," *Library Trends* 52, no. 1 (Summer 2004): 112–28, https://www.ideals.illinois.edu/ bitstream/handle/2142/1716/Bernfeld112128.pdf?sequence=2.
3. Singer Group, "The 5 Practices of Progressive Leaders," February 12, 2013, www.singergrp.com/blog/2013/02/12/the-5-practices-of-progressive-leaders/.
4. Plato, *Plato: The Complete Works*, ed. John M. Cooper (Indianapolis, IN: Hackett, 1997), 1008–15.
5. Robert R. Leichtman and Carl Japikse, *The Art of Living* (Columbus, OH: Arial, 1986), (Vol 5) p. 85.
6. David K. Williams, "Great Leaders Know Respect Is the Keystone of a Successful Business," *Forbes Entrepreneurs Magazine*, May 29, 2013, www.forbes.com/sites/david kwilliams/2013/05/29/great-leaders-know-respect-is-the-keystone-of-a-successful -business/#3e7ae4d3452e.

Six

THINK THINGS THROUGH

What we think, we become.

BUDDHA

N o treatment of how libraries invigorate communities would be complete without the investigation of how to strengthen and sustain our ability to think and act responsibly. Some of us working in libraries practice the "art" of acting before thinking, while others concentrate on preserving their comfort and avoiding accountability. Still others personalize their work and become sidetracked when community members criticize the library. Why create barriers to the practice of treasuring those we serve? Let's learn to think things through effectively.

For example, a librarian creates an ambitious series of programs to reach out to a specific segment of the community—at-risk families, young entrepreneurs, or artists. But the project takes too much time, and soon other responsibilities are neglected. Although the program series is important and worthwhile, the lesson to be learned is to think things through during the planning process in order to determine a reasonable amount of time, effort, and funding to devote to the project before implementing it. This scenario is true not only for program planning, but also for collection development, service delivery, or any attempt to do something new—*think it through!*

How can libraries create new programs without ignoring the purpose of libraries to enlighten humanity? A worst-case business example of an organization straying too far from its purpose was J.C. Penney. The company, known for its discount prices for clothing, made a series of decisions without appearing to ask what's working well. During a seventeen-month period from 2011 to 2013, a century of success was nearly shattered. A new CEO from a tech company—with good intentions—introduced several new business strategies, but did not think things through. Although the strategies had been successful at the tech company, they did not fit J. C. Penney, a retail company. Thousands of top-notch middle managers and hundreds of headquarters staff—who understood the clothing retail business—were laid off. The company lost its retail savviness and its ability to make useful decisions. It could not evaluate what was working well and what was not. Its long-time advertising company was fired, and the logo was changed three times in three years. A complicated new pricing structure was established. J.C. Penney stores across the country were forced to create "mini-shops" for other companies, like Levi's and Martha Stewart products. The message we should take away from this is: *although change will be a keystone to a library's ability to invigorate the community, thoughtful and intelligent change is far more likely to firmly establish ongoing success.*

Shakespeare's Hamlet asserts in act II, "There is nothing either good or bad, but thinking makes it so." He is making a point about the value of staying above the fray. An experience or event is neither positive nor negative until we determine which it will be. For example, a library misjudges the impact of service changes and is heavily criticized in news media and social media. The stories become overblown. But if we stay above the fray and embrace the situation as a golden opportunity, we can get busy finding the right solution. We can take what starts out as a negative and turn it into a positive.

If colleagues view outside criticism as a discouraging event, help them to think it through and take it in stride. It's the same event whether viewed constructively or destructively. Let's take the positive approach! Why not turn a sudden problem into an unexpected opportunity for the organization to grow and learn together?

MAKING ROOM FOR THE NEW—WITHOUT DESTROYING WHAT WORKS WELL

A key to making room for the "new" is to ponder what's working well, what's not working, and what we can do differently to be more effective in the long run. If you approach the improvement of library service using a big-picture

FIGURE 6.1

Adding to traditional print picture book collections, many libraries offer early literacy interactions using touchscreens.

Photo: Courtesy of Harford County (MD) Public Library

view, you are more likely to grasp the needs of the community as a whole. Libraries that thrive are geared toward asking how to help the community in order to bolster all elements, so that—as the saying goes—all boats rise. "It's a matter of course to work together, the library and the community. The key is to let people know what we do and can do," says Irene Padilla, Maryland state librarian.

Canceling a successful program may or may not demonstrate a thoughtful approach. Significant changes may or may not improve a service that has been working well. How can we know when change is needed? How do we know when a simple tweak or two will ramp up a questionable service—or if we need to drop it to make room for a new service? What are the signals to stay the course for positive long-term results? Let's weave together the right attitude, useful questions, and broad thinking in order to make the best decision today and thereby produce effective results that last 10, 20, or even 50 years.

Decision-making involves integrating organizational values, priorities, and goals. In the 1990s, many libraries established a priority based on the community need to support parents and caregivers in their role as first teachers. The Carroll County Public Library began a new training program for early childhood educators that stretched over three consecutive Saturday mornings, with assignments for participants in between sessions. The training was extremely popular with the early childhood education community, but it was time-consuming for library staff members to plan, prepare, and deliver. They asked questions:

- Can we reduce the number of training hours, yet retain the high-quality content? *Yes!*
- Will most educators continue to take the training despite a reduction of credit hours? *Yes!* (*They did.*)
- Can we offer the same training several times in a row to avoid the time-intensive process of starting from scratch with a new topic? *Of course!*
- Will we reach a large number of educators on each topic? *Yes!*

The training transitioned from ten hours over three consecutive Saturdays to an eight-hour training offered on two Saturdays—four hours each day—with a free weekend in between. As an example of ongoing evaluation, library staff have upped the ante in recent years by offering six hours each Saturday instead of four hours. The program's long-term impact—now fifteen years after the original training—demonstrates the value of thinking things through:

- The library has trained several hundred educators on topics of early literacy, math, science, social and emotional development, and the importance of learning through play.
- The library has indirectly reached several thousand children and their parents and caregivers.
- Library staff time for the training project was reduced, allowing more time to drive bookmobiles, perform puppet shows, and serve the community in other ways.
- The reduced workload helped avoid staff burnout and the potentially low morale to follow.
- Participants appreciated the two-Saturday solution for easier scheduling on their part.
- A span of two weeks in between workshops allowed for more flexibility to apply the training with the children in their classrooms and complete training assignments.
- Through word-of-mouth promotion, educators flock to register, enjoy the quality training, and appreciate earning twelve clock hours—two additional hours compared to the original ten hours.

Libraries may find themselves in a position where most things are working well, and the only way to grow and change is to completely drop something even though it's at the height of its success. As long as library administrators and staffers think through the process, they can determine how to move

FIGURE 6.2

Training early childhood educators is a top priority for many libraries. A key to long-term success is to ask questions, such as what's working well and what we can do differently to be more effective. Workshops can become a magnet for educators to flock to the library for learning, networking, and activating creative thinking.

Photo: Courtesy of Carroll County (MD) Public Library

forward with long-term results in mind. The answer may be to reduce service or offer a program less frequently instead of dropping it.

Opportunities to make room for the "new" sometimes happen unexpectedly due to a resignation or other type of staffing shift. The Denton (TX) Public Library collaborated with local government, schools, businesses, and other organizations to produce a monthly television show to educate children about the community. After five years, the popular and award-winning production—which featured an entertaining bevy of puppet characters—ended. The decision to sunset Library Larry's Big Day television show was taken not because it was doing poorly, but because a key member of the production crew resigned in order to stay home with a growing family. The library thought through several options, including finding a replacement, but decided to free up production crew time in order to explore and discover other community needs.

The Denton library purchased a small library-to-go van to continue its core value of spreading services in the community. The van stores a few tables and chairs, a lawn umbrella, bins of programming materials, and free books to give away—allowing these outreach champions to set up anywhere, anytime, indoors or outside. From music, art, and early literacy programs to hands-on science, math, and technology activities for all ages, library staffers connect people who are isolated, underserved, or unaware of library services. Slowly

FIGURE 6.3

Denton Public Library to Go!

Photo: Courtesy of Denton (TX)
Public Library

FIGURE 6.4

Denton Public Library to Go! connects library services to community enclaves.

Photo: Courtesy of Denton (TX)
Public Library

but steadily over an eighteen-month period, tweaking each step of the way, the service has grown. The team transformed their outreach efforts to reach sites ranging from grocery stores, farmers' markets, and parks to retirement communities, food banks, and facilities for adults with learning disabilities.

The Pikes Peake Library director John Spears says, "Occasionally, the only way to respond to the community effectively and in a timely way is to be open to stopping a program while it is on a high note. Otherwise, the organization may not be able to fulfill an emerging community need or try something new." Joseph Thompson, the Carroll County Public Library director of public services and Reference & User Services Association president (2014–15), adds, "Making changes effectively is a process: *carefully judge what to drop, tweak, or change without losing sight of the library's purpose.*"

What can libraries give up, reduce, or modify in order to make room for more hands-on maker activities? Jen Bishop, the emerging technologies and online services supervisor at the Carroll County Library, developed an idea for an interactive display kit called CRATE—Create Reinvent Apply Teach Explore—for library branches to make available at a table on the public floor during all hours of operation. "What we needed was the ability to reach more people than we had been doing through scheduled programs," says Bishop. A generous grant from the Association for Library Services to Children and the Disney corporation afforded the opportunity to pilot a set of rotating kits to every library branch and the outreach department. Within a four-month period, the library anticipated 650 people taking advantage of the CRATE stations. However, an amazing 4,200 children, teens, and adults participated

FIGURE 6.5

Strawbees interactive station or CRATE (Create Reinvent Apply Teach Explore), Eldersburg Branch, Carroll County (MD) Public Library.

Photo: Courtesy of Carroll County (MD) Public Library

FIGURE 6.6

The Colorado Springs Mini Maker Faire brings dozens of makers and thousands of attendees to Library 21c each year.

Photo: Courtesy of Pikes Peak (CO) Library District's Library 21c

in the activities, such as Strawbees, robotics, and electrical circuitry. After the grant, the library has continued to fund new kits, rotating them among branch locations. *Staff who can determine what will have staying power in the long run help the library thrive!*

In recent years, the American Library Association's "Libraries Transform" initiative partnered with the Harwood Institute for Public Innovation to create a toolbox of strategies for libraries to actively support the communities they serve. Columbus, Wisconsin, a small town of 5,000 people, had been struggling financially. But in recent years, a growing Madison commuter population has been giving the area an economic boost. The library has adopted Harwood's "Turning Outward" strategy of the library as a neutral convener—leading discussion programs to help bridge the gap between new and old elements of the town.

Cindy Fesemyer, the Columbus library director, says, "Library staff members take the neutral stance in our Community Conversations and aim to bring out the best in people in order to build trust among the town's new and old guard." Some examples of Harwood questions to encourage discussion in order to find commonalities among residents are:

- What kind of community do you want live in?
- Why is that important to you?
- How is that different than what is in your community now?
- What are some of the things that need to happen to create that kind of change?

Benjamin Franklin was a master of thinking things through—for long-term results. He established a public library, fire department, and community hospital in Philadelphia. He brought wisdom to foreign diplomacy, insight (and humor) to intensive debates, and practical suggestions that helped transform a group of colonies into a united country.

The Library Company of Philadelphia, founded in 1731 by Franklin, is now an outstanding research library specializing in American history and culture from the seventeenth through the nineteenth centuries. A working copy of the U.S. Constitution in the library's collection demonstrates Franklin's ability to think things through thoroughly and completely. The draft manuscript reads: "We the People of the States of New Hampshire, Massachusetts, Rhode Island and Providence Plantations, Connecticut, New York, New Jersey, Pennsylvania, Delaware, Maryland, Virginia, North

FIGURE 6.7

Benjamin Franklin, a copy by Anne Leslie from the original portrait by the French artist J. S. Duplessis when Franklin was in Paris.

Source: Library Company of Philadelphia

Carolina, South Carolina, and Georgia, do ordain, declare, and establish the following Constitution for the Government of Ourselves and our Property." In Franklin's handwriting, the names of the states are crossed out in his working document with the word "United" scribbled in front of the word "States" to read: "We the People of the United States."

Creating a public library—or what was known as the Library Company—was a natural extension of Franklin's need to read widely in order to enhance discussion and expand the mind. He and his friends were centuries ahead of their time in their encouragement of informal education for women. The Library Company can document women's use of the collection as early as 1746.

Franklin believed in reason as a pathway for the steady and continuous growth of humanity. As a young man he formed a Junto, a group of tradesmen and professionals focused on self-improvement. In 1728 Franklin established a list of rules for his club, which had been organized "for mutual improvement." A few examples from the list, when slightly modified, can easily apply to us today. How can librarians invigorate themselves and those they serve?

- Have you met anything in the author you last read, remarkable or suitable, to be communicated? particularly in demonstrating respect and goodwill, in poetry and cultural arts, travel, technology, science, history, or other parts of knowledge?

- Can you think of anything at present, in which librarians may be serviceable to humankind, to their community, to their friends, or to themselves?
- What new story have you lately heard that is agreeable for telling in conversation?
- Do you know of any deserving young thinker, whom it lies in the power of the library in any way to encourage?
- Have you lately heard of any citizen's thriving well, and by what means?

Franklin and his colleagues sought to bring out the best in themselves and each other in order to improve their community. To join the group, members made a pledge:

1. Have you any particular disrespect to any present members? **Answer:** *I have not.*
2. Do you sincerely declare that you love humanity in general, of what profession or religion soever? **Answer:** *I do.*
3. Do you think persons ought to be harmed in their bodies, names, or goods, for mere speculative opinions, or their external way of worship? **Answer:** *No.*
4. Do you love truth for truth's sake, and will you endeavor impartially to find and receive it yourself, and communicate it to others? **Answer:** *Yes.*[1]

The edits that Benjamin Franklin scribbled on his draft copy of the Constitution suggest that he and others thought things through. It's one reason why the U.S. Constitution is still around. The idea was to think through the business at hand and inspire upon the original purpose. Libraries today can think things through—thoroughly and completely—and bring out the best in our organizations and communities—for all to thrive for years to come.

NOTE

1. Adapted from Benjamin Franklin, *The Autobiography & Other Writings by Benjamin Franklin*, ed. Peter Shaw (New York: Bantam Books, 1982), 195–97.

PART III

BECOME AN OUTSTANDING LIBRARY LEADER

Seven

CARNEGIE'S LIGHT

How far that little candle throws his beam!

WILLIAM SHAKESPEARE

" will put you on the spot where your qualifications as a leader will be shown up for precisely what they are,"[1] said Andrew Carnegie, nineteenth-century industrialist, philanthropist, and grantor of 1,689 American libraries and over 800 additional libraries worldwide. Speaking to a protégé, Carnegie articulated several life principles: go the extra mile, do to others what you want them to do to you, and do not become over-impressed with your own importance. Other gems include: understand your role and purpose, develop a helpful mental attitude, seek inspiration, make yourself indispensable in your job, do your own thinking, exercise self-discipline, and cultivate creative vision.

In this section we'll explore some of these principles as connected to the purpose of a library. We'll learn how the principles helped Carnegie spawn modern philanthropy and the concept of charitable organizations. More specifically, we'll discover how he transformed the public library from a closed stack, subscription-based book repository into a community anchor focused on uplifting humanity.

Many of us in the library field may not realize the stunning leadership of Andrew Carnegie in creating the modern public library or why it is important to our work today. What do we think of when we hear Carnegie's name? We may know that a century ago "Carnegie grants" offered communities the ability to fund a library building. The Carnegie Corporation's ongoing support for libraries can be seen today through its sponsorship of distinguished awards in collaboration with the American Library Association. We may be aware of the Andrew Carnegie Medal for notable children's videos, and the Andrew Carnegie Medals for Excellence for fiction and nonfiction books. In addition, the Carnegie-Whitney grant may be familiar to us. It supports the preparation of popular or scholarly reading lists, webliographies, indexes, and other guides to library resources that will be useful to patrons and customers of all types of libraries in the United States.[2]

Most of us are busy delivering and creating customer service experiences and don't think about Carnegie. In some circles, it may be an automatic response to disparage Andrew Carnegie when his name is mentioned. In other camps, although praise is given for his largesse, it is followed by disapproval of his business ability. Some naysayers believe that he treated his workers poorly, then felt guilty and gave away his money. The copious evidence suggests otherwise.

Andrew Carnegie immigrated to the Pittsburgh, Pennsylvania, area from Scotland in 1848 at the age of thirteen. In school textbooks and classrooms of the 1960s in western Pennsylvania, Andrew Carnegie was praised for his generosity. His spirit of giving was apparent in the "Carnegie" libraries in the region, Carnegie-Mellon University, and the magnificent Carnegie Museum of Pittsburgh that continues to host one of the finest dinosaur fossil collections in the world. However, a dark cloud hung over Carnegie's name in class discussion because he was termed a "robber baron." What is a robber baron?

The term "robber baron" was first used in the medieval era to describe landowning nobles or barons who overcharged travelers passing over land or along the rivers adjacent to their property. Carnegie did not live during medieval times. In the nineteenth and early twentieth centuries, the term "robber baron" resurfaced and was used by muckraking journalists to describe people who invested in companies with the sole purpose of making profits, no matter if the company was destroyed in the process. Carnegie was the opposite of this definition of a robber baron. He turned his company into the best steelmaking enterprise in the world. Like many thriving companies today—and many libraries—he believed that higher wages were a good investment for "men who respect their employers and are happy and contented . . . yielding, indeed, big dividends."[3] You pay the right person a decent wage, and in return he performs his duties well, which benefits the company. Carnegie perfected the Bessemer steelmaking technology, which greatly reduced costs to the consumer and encouraged railroad companies to choose steel for their rails. It was a thriving business.

The genius of Carnegie's life principles is that they can apply to everyone. Surplus money—funds left over after the satisfying needs and wants of an individual and family—is eligible to give away for the betterment of society. Carnegie's philanthropic philosophy focused not only on millionaires, but on "everyone who has but a small surplus above his [basic needs and] moderate wants."[4] He described the giving away of surplus money as a duty to be administered carefully for the good of the people.

The core of Carnegie's philanthropic philosophy was to award a construction grant only to those communities that were willing to sustain a new library's funding for at least ten years and pay for its staffing, operation, and collection development. The community's financial commitment was usually made through local taxes. Carnegie made an exception to this rule early on, giving an endowment to four cities instead of requiring local support. A study by Roger Munn appeared in *Library Journal* in 1951 showing that those four cities were the only Carnegie libraries without local support. Those four libraries offered few services and did not grow their endowments. This scenario helps demonstrate the potential of healthy reciprocity in collaboration: if the library engages the community and serves it well, the community invests well in the library, and thus helps its members thrive.

Carnegie focused on working with communities that understood charity as a leg up for someone who is willing to help him or herself. Libraries offered the opportunity for self-education, and constant inspiration to be one's best. Carnegie wrote to one candidate applying for a library building grant: "I believe that it outranks any other one thing that a community can do to benefit its people. It is the never failing spring in the desert."[5]

We cannot afford to understate Carnegie's leadership and how it applies to today's libraries. He led the way above and beyond granting funds to construct buildings. "In our work to support libraries, the Knight Foundation harks back to Carnegie. He challenged libraries to stop thinking about the past. He placed an emphasis on exploring the technologies of the day. He pushed libraries into the future," says John Bracken, vice-president of media innovation at the Knight Foundation. Carnegie turned his fortune into a library legacy that continues to help communities flourish today.

After Carnegie sold his steel company, he applied his organizational skill, brilliance, and hard work to finding the "best uses to devote [his] surpluses."

He committed the majority of his efforts to the institution of the library. Within one generation, from the 1890s to 1920, Carnegie reinvented the public library.

Although many Carnegie library buildings in use today are poorly designed for handling today's robust services and programs, the principles behind Carnegie's library vision apply more now than ever. Can libraries enlighten humanity—as Carnegie envisioned? Yes! Can librarians apply Carnegie's principles of the art of living? Absolutely! We can practice the principles: go the extra mile, treat others the way we'd like to be treated, and avoid becoming over-impressed with our own importance. By thinking things through, we are better able to gain insight into our role and purpose, and to seek inspiration and apply enthusiasm in serving our communities.

Let's not deny that Carnegie did a great service to the world in helping people of all walks of life to cultivate their minds. Those working in today's libraries should be trumpeting his remarkable vision and accomplishment from the top of every library—no matter if it is a "Carnegie" library or not.

Can we hold libraries to higher standards of honesty, integrity, and truth? Can we rise to Carnegie's principles to cultivate creative vision and capture the essence of mind development? Can libraries carry Carnegie's torch as a guiding light to help individuals be their best and help humanity—to develop a helpful mental attitude and become more forgiving and tolerant?

According to Tim Brown, CEO and president of the international design consulting firm IDEO and the author of *Change by Design*, the answer is yes!

FIGURE 7.1

Carnegie Library of Pittsburgh, Main Branch (built in 1895). Carnegie believed that education and literature were not luxuries for the affluent, but rather tools to improve the minds of everyone. That explains the promise adorning many Carnegie's libraries: "Free to the People." Are libraries living up to this motto and to the philosophy that libraries offer an avenue to improve the mind?

Photo: takomabibelot, http://farm3.staticflickr.com/2364/2139542438_067407c689_z.jpg

FIGURE 7.2

The newly remodeled Thomas Hughes Children's Area, Harold Washington Library Center, Chicago Public Library, offers customized learning experiences for early learners, elementary learners and tweens.

Photo: D. Stoltz

Creative vision always benefits from an abundance of inspiration. The more we can express this creative vision, the more the community benefits. The library offers an abundance of inspiration for all: not only for those who cannot afford books, but for those who have all the money in the world. Brian Bannon, commissioner of the Chicago Public Library, adds, "We are excited about our vision and mission to serve the community. One of our biggest assets is experimentation while exercising patience around the constraints we face. We are constantly thinking about how to improve and how to make room for creativity. Our goal is to help uplift the community a day at a time, a person at a time."

Knowing an organization's purpose and one's role in it can help an individual develop a mature pride in his or her work. People who celebrate their accomplishments each step of the way are more likely to persist in overcoming difficult tasks. They strengthen their abilities and produce long-term results. Achievement—and its celebration—creates a wavelength of gratitude, persistence, and optimism.

As an example, Henry Ford, twentieth-century engineer, businessman, and founder of the Ford Motor Company, transformed American industry and revolutionized transportation. He perfected the assembly line and consequently made automobiles much more than a lavish curiosity; they became an integral part of modern life and put America on wheels. After seeing a steam-propelled tractor, a seed was planted in Ford's mind about the possibility of a horseless buggy. He nurtured this idea and kept his mind charged with the purpose of the emerging automobile industry—to make transportation more efficient and affordable. He continually sought to find ways to convey the power of the internal-combustion engine to the wheels of a vehicle.

Ford sought the counsel of a group of smart, hard-working people who had experimented with internal-combustion engines, transmissions, and other mechanical applications. They were willing to invest their time, expertise, and money in Ford's vision. Over time—one step at a time and overcoming many obstacles—his purpose translated into plans and into action. Carnegie said, "If one quality stands out about Ford, above all others, it is his capacity for persistence."[6]

A survey, "The 7 Key Trends Impacting Today's Workplace," was conducted by TINYpulse in 2014, and involved over 200,000 employees in more than 500 organizations. The question, "What motivates you to excel and go the extra mile at your organization?" brought this popular response: intrinsic desire [and enthusiasm] to [do] a good job.[7] Carnegie relied on the principle of what he called "seek inspiration (enthusiasm applied)." Implicit in this principle is the art of striving to be one's best.

What does it mean to be one's best?

- Strive to excel but avoid any tendency to be a perfectionist.
- Be inspired using quiet enthusiasm.
- Practice integrity, gracefulness, and patience.
- Persevere!

By striving to be one's best, a person learns to discipline the use of emotion—transmuting negative emotions such as fear, anger, and distrust, into the expression of positive emotions such as love, optimism, and gratitude. Additionally, the superb skill of *exercising self-discipline* helps produce positive results and creates an underlying—yet strong and steady—reservoir of quiet enthusiasm and optimism. These qualities help drive perseverance.

Do libraries create cultures in which their staff members can practice being their best? Do libraries encourage customers to work at their best?

Seth Goldman and Barry Nalebuff, coauthors of *Mission in a Bottle: The Honest Guide to Doing Business Differently—and Succeeding*, are examples of entrepreneurs who are practicing many of Carnegie's principles. As outsiders to the beverage industry, Goldman, a former student, and Nalebuff, a professor, cofounded Honest Tea. The name itself is a pun on "honesty"—which is lacking in too many businesses! They *cultivated a creative vision* to design a tasty beverage with reduced sugar that is low in calories—what you see on the label is what you get.

In 1997, Goldman puzzled over finding something he wanted to drink at the store after jogging in Central Park, New York City. Although the range and type of beverages on the shelf were plentiful—and excellent for many people's taste—the offerings were too sweet for Goldman. This was Goldman's eureka moment: why not produce a beverage that he—and probably others—would enjoy?

Goldman called Nalebuff, his former business professor, to discuss the potential of designing, producing, and marketing a new beverage—together. Unbeknownst to Goldman, Nalebuff had taken a trip to India in 1997 to write a case study about a company that produced a better quality tea than the type of tea offered in the United States. Their conversations quickly led to what Carnegie regarded as *understanding role and purpose*. Their mutual interest in exploring a new product strengthened their bond from student and teacher to CEO and chairman. Goldman took the lead and became CEO—or as he describes his role using another pun, "Tea-EO." Nalebuff took on the role of a chairman focused on helping Goldman to be successful. Their primary purpose was to provide a great-tasting, honest, healthy drink.

Working out of his home kitchen, Goldman brewed, bottled, and began promoting the new beverage. Although the tea began to sell to small stores in the local area, he encountered several obstacles. Goldman, who was new to truck driving, made deliveries himself using a rented truck. He accidentally damaged the top of the truck one day by driving it into a parking garage with a low entrance. Shortly thereafter, Goldman met with a big-name distributor that offered discouraging feedback: your tea is not sweet enough, it tastes grassy, and it's too expensive.

Goldman applied Carnegie's principle of using a *helpful mental attitude* to stay above the fray and figure out his next steps. He persevered by seeking distributors that could help with deliveries to smaller outlets, such as gourmet cheese shops. He managed to arrange a meeting with a large grocery store whose buyer not only liked the drink, but immediately placed an order for 15,000 bottles. Goldman and Nalebuff—unable to handle such an order out of Goldman's kitchen—quickly contracted with a beverage bottling company to fill their first major order. Twenty years after its formation, the company continues to grow and expand by creating new beverage products, such as an organic kids' drink and an organic sports drink. Goldman continues to innovate in food through his involvement in a new company, Beyond Meat, which has created a tastier plant-based burger. The original investors in

FIGURE 7.3

Seth Goldman, entrepreneur and author, on right, spreading the light of enthusiasm, honesty, and going the extra mile with a Carroll Community College business student in Maryland.

Photo: Kati Hoffman

Honest Tea have earned twenty-six times their money. Goldman emphasizes, "This was not an overnight success . . . and we worked our tails off."[8]

As Tea-EO of Honest Tea, Goldman was forced to be indispensable, otherwise his company would fail. He wasn't trained to drive a big vehicle, and so he initially wasn't cognizant of overpasses and garage heights. However, he learned the hard way not only how to handle driving a truck, but how to brew outstanding tea, market it, distribute it, make payroll, and overcome personal and professional challenges. He learned how to rely on honesty to make Honest Tea and thrive.

Do libraries sell "honesty" to our patrons? Some people may think that honesty doesn't have a place in libraries. But as Carnegie understood, libraries are not just about collections, programs, technology, and services; they are a community portal for cultivating beauty, honesty, and the larger use of the mind.

Carnegie did not ask for the libraries he funded to be adorned by his name. However, he did request—which was not always filled—to incorporate the phrase, "Let There Be Light."

To Carnegie, understanding a situation thoroughly was the fulfillment of the phrase, "let there be light." He was fond of a pre-Civil War story that illustrated this. The judge in the story represented the repulsive attitude of white people at that time. The judge had a great deal to learn and to unlearn about his bigotry and prejudice. One day he asked a runaway slave, "You had a good, kind master, you were not overworked, plenty to eat, good clothes, fine

FIGURE 7.4

The Edinburgh Central Library, which is considered to be Carnegie's finest and most important library in Scotland. Written above the entrance is the proclamation: "Let There Be Light" over a rising sun, with foliage to left and right. The Central Library (built in 1887) was considered to be a beacon of enlightenment. How often do libraries view themselves as a guiding light?

Photo: Joanna Paterson, https://www.flickr.com/photos/joanna_young/2424017026

home. I don't see why the devil you wished to run away." The runaway slave replied, "Well Judge, I left my position open. You can go down and take it." According to Carnegie, the judge was then able to see a great *light*.[9]

This anecdote follows Carnegie's library motto: let there be light. In the drive for freedom among black people, the judge was able to see the truth of slavery. The institution of the library similarly reveals a great light. Those of us working in libraries should live up to it. Every library job today is made possible by Andrew Carnegie's understanding of the library's potential. Let's celebrate Carnegie's light!

NOTES

1. Napoleon Hill, *Napoleon Hill's The Wisdom of Andrew Carnegie as Told to Napoleon Hill* (Wise, VA: Napoleon Hill Foundation, 2004), 148.

2. American Library Association, www.ala.org/offices/publishing/sundry/alapubawrds/carnegiewhitney.

3. Andrew Carnegie, *Autobiography of Andrew Carnegie* (1920; Las Vegas, NV: Lits, 2011), 121.

4. Andrew Carnegie, *The Gospel of Wealth* (1901; Atlanta, GA: Kudzu House, 2008), 90.

5. Joseph Frazier Wall, *Andrew Carnegie* (Pittsburgh, PA: University of Pittsburgh Press, 1989), 818–19.

6. Hill, *Napoleon Hill's The Wisdom of Andrew Carnegie*, 162.

7. Victor Lipman, "New Study Answers: What Motivates Employees to 'Go the Extra Mile?'" *Forbes*, November 4, 2014, https://www.forbes.com/sites/victorlipman/2014/11/04/what-motivates-employees-to-go-the-extra-mile-study-offers-surprising-answer/#3a244231a055.

8. Seth Goldman and Barry Nalebuff, *Mission in a Bottle: The Honest Guide to Doing Business Differently—and Succeeding* (New York: Crown Business, 2013), 264.

9. Adapted from Carnegie, *Autobiography of Andrew Carnegie*, 182–83.

Eight

GETTING EVERYONE ON THE RIGHT PAGE

*Teamwork is the ability to work together toward a common vision;
this is the ability to direct individual accomplishment toward
organizational objectives. It is the fuel that allows common people
to attain uncommon results.*

ANDREW CARNEGIE

L ibrary work increasingly focuses on a new kind of collaboration in which staff across departments support common activities defined by a strong director. This is a different kind of collaboration than the trend of the last twenty years. First, the pendulum of change swung from a common scenario of the *director as a visionary guiding the team* to a weaker scenario of administrators, middle managers, and front-line staffers as collective visionaries directing the director. Was there a time when some library directors made decisions without input from staff and produced poor results? Yes! Did some directors exaggerate their power, stifling creativity among staff? Absolutely! But do those rare occasions diminish the director or devalue the effort of the director to get everyone on the same page? No!

Although input from all levels of staff—a collaborative approach—can be important in helping a director or CEO make wise decisions, it can also be overdone. This is especially true when employees mistakenly believe the organization is supposed to be a democracy and they consider their vote or opinion as having equal or nearly equal weight to the director's. These staffers may not realize that it is helpful to think from the director's perspective—and to do all they can do to make the director proud. The top position is designed to act as a portal for receiving, interpreting, and passing library purpose and inspiration down through the organization.

Staffers inspire the director. They are often more knowledgeable about specific service deliveries than the director and may be more creative and skilled at the day-to-day work. However, the role of the director is to rally the troops and get everyone on the right page—the same page as the director. The best directors across the country lead their staff. They do not follow staffers who have momentary interests or personal causes that would lead to poor service or disrupt community goodwill. They take a neutral stance that allows all community members to turn to the library for inspiration.

Strong library directors demonstrate daily to staff and community members what it means to be one's best—promoting tolerance, goodwill, and cheerfulness. As Thomas Jefferson stated in a letter to William Hamilton on April 22, 1800: *I never considered a difference of opinion in politics, in religion, in philosophy, as a cause for withdrawing from a friend.*[1]

Strong directors create a "page"—an inspired page in the book of life—that embraces the purpose of the library as enlightening society. They may think of it as: how can the library bring out the best in the community we serve?

A crucial time for a leader to exercise his or her strength and ability is in the face of adversity. Winston Churchill, Britain's prime minister during World War II, shone as an extraordinary leader because he motivated the British people to defend themselves against the Nazis. His determination, perseverance, and devotion towards the nation sparked people to go forward and win the war with the help of their Allies. He won not only the war but the hearts of millions of people with his courage, common sense, and optimism. Although the words "Keep Calm and Carry On" are not Churchill's, they are associated with his spirit and his leadership in a time of crisis.[2] Churchill's favorite maxims during the war were actually "Keep Plodding On" and "Keep Buggering On." He often shortened these phrases to KPO or KBO and started and ended his very long days declaring: "We must just KBO."[3]

The director position holds the key to understanding and conveying library purpose throughout the organization and in the community. Eddie Rickenbacker, the first president of Eastern Air Lines in the 1930s, successfully understood and conveyed his new industry's purpose—to get people flying. Eastern quickly grew into a top-performing, highly innovative company, which it remained until the 1960s, when Rickenbacker's successors did not stay focused on the big-picture view of the industry and disregarded his inspiring tone that kept employees on the same page. The company declined.

The director may have a general plan in mind on how to enlighten humanity through library services and programs. This plan may not move in a straight

FIGURE 8.1

"Keep Calm and Carry On" poster created by the British government, 1939.

line from A to B to C, but from A to S to E, depending on the appearance of opportunities. Do staffers implement the library director's plan? Do senior staff members understand the director's plan? Let's explore how to get staff on the right page—the director's page—and demonstrate how to find an effective balance between a strong director and brave and tenacious followers, who are leaders in their own right.

COOPERATION

The act of cooperation doesn't mean, "I'm on top! You do what I think should be done." Unfortunately, this attitude prevails in society today. We may think we know about cooperation and collaboration, but we usually know very little of their true meanings, and about how to put these concepts into action in order to benefit the organization and ultimately the community we serve.

Many people embrace the erroneous notion that cooperation means they can dictate exactly what others should be doing. This kind of "cooperation" becomes coercion of the work group. Calling it cooperation doesn't make it so. We cannot assume that senior staff members have actually mastered cooperation. Getting staff to be on the same page starts with the fundamentals of knowing the library's purpose, the role of the director, and the part that each unit plays, and with staff members embracing these fundamentals.

The word "cooperation," stemming from the Late Latin word *cooperari*, translates to "working together." *Operari* can be defined as "to have effect, be active." These words are tied to "synergy," emerging from the Greek *synergia* or "joint work, cooperation; assistance, help."

Correctly applied, synergy brings out the best in ourselves and others. However, it is not a blissful process of agreeing with everyone on every issue. In fact, a savvy director does not want a group of "yes men" (or women). A successful senior team helps a director make decisions, brings discernment and intellectual criticism to the table, and questions assumptions and perceptions—but once the director issues a policy, the team supports it.

Effective cooperation does not necessarily mean being comfortable or "feeling good" about all decisions. It doesn't matter whether you "like" the members on your team. It certainly doesn't matter whether you listen to the same music or have the same political beliefs. It is sometimes—and perhaps often—the case that someone in your organization whom you don't, at first, think you'll get along with turns out to be the person you learn the most from. Indeed, that person may lead you to a different, not-to-be-missed perspective or deeper level of thinking that turns a good service into a great service.

THE DIRECTOR'S CONNECTION TO LIBRARY PURPOSE

When a director understands what Franklin and Carnegie understood—that the library's broad purpose is to enlighten humanity—he or she can direct common individual accomplishment toward organizational objectives and attain "uncommon results." "To create an effective, motivated, and joyful team, a leader must build on the skills and strengths of each staff member and figure out how to get them to work together," says Susan Hildreth, professor of practice at the University of Washington's Information School and former director of the Institute for Museums and Libraries. Taken as a group, library staffers are a bevy of individuals who need to be molded into a single unit. Babe Ruth said, "The way the team plays as a whole determines its success. You may have the greatest bunch of individual stars in the world, but if they don't play together, the club won't be worth a dime."

The director can appreciate their individuality and let staff members develop. He or she needs individuals, but the director needs them to work together without destroying their individuality. At the same time, the director should not reward faux individuality, that is, a person who succumbs to predigested cultural beliefs conflicting with library purpose. All staff members need to get on board with the director's page if they are to work in the library.

Everyone learns to articulate the library's purpose but also works to fulfill it—and does nothing to sabotage it. Getting on the same page means all staff not sabotaging the directions that come from above. Some staff use a pocket veto of the boss; they don't implement or only partially implement the instructions. Such behavior can undermine and even cripple the ability of the organization to succeed.

When directors understand that the library is meant to encourage people to think and grow—perhaps without quite realizing it—all their energy goes toward achieving that end. As the library hires people, they are selected based not only on whether they can do the work required, but also on whether they can fulfill the broader purpose of a library in society—helping humanity to strive to be its best. Children's librarians are hired to present storytimes and support parents in their role as first teacher, in order for children to develop a foundation for inspired learning. Teen services librarians are expected to develop hands-on activities to get students excited about reading and learn to think things through as a means to enrich life. Adult services staff are skilled in working with individuals, businesses, and organizations to help people improve their discernment skills and contribute more to the community. Outreach librarians are hired to serve struggling families who don't use the library, to reach out to the homeless, the incarcerated, and the elderly—in order to spark their curiosity through reading and to provide activities that lift them up.[4]

Is your organization willing to allow the director to mold individuals into a great team? Like preparing a soup recipe, a great chef knows how to stir the pot, for how long, and at what temperature and when to add a pinch of salt, a sprig of thyme, and a zest of lemon. Does your library have a shared respect for all of your established—and potential—customers? Are there team members who use the library for personal causes and inadvertently belittle some of your customers? Do these team members need a pinch of humility, a sprig of tolerance, and a zest of cheerfulness?

There isn't a better example of synergy in a group of diverse individuals than the one created by Abraham Lincoln in naming his often stormy presidential cabinet.[5]

Lincoln carefully assembled a group that would be representative of all conflicting viewpoints in the country at that time—people who wanted to free the slaves, those who wanted to keep slavery in the South, those who advocated not to expand slavery to new territories, and those who promoted secession of the southern states. In Lincoln's book, getting people on the same page meant keeping the country together.

Lincoln not only stayed above the fray of political infighting, but also refused to become a sloppy thinker. After the Union's defeat at the first Battle of Bull Run, Walt Whitman observed Lincoln refusing to surrender to the

gloom of failure: "He unflinchingly stemm'd it, and resolv'd to lift himself and the Union out of it."[6] The brilliance of Lincoln's ability to understand his role in keeping the country together and to think things through set the stage for a dynamic atmosphere in which his disparate cabinet could cooperate and work together. It is an important lesson for library administrators to lead and develop courageous followers, who are strong leaders but still exemplify the concept of being on the same page—the director's page.

In making sure that his cabinet reflected the diverse viewpoints of the nation, Lincoln was clearly bringing a potential for dissension, insubordination, or even sabotage close to him. He knew that the best way to deal with these problems was to keep them close at hand, in order to deal with them before they arose. These people could better understand his decisions and why he was doing what he did, each step of the way.

COURAGEOUS FOLLOWERS

Talking about and establishing core values have become popular today in many organizations. Posting the list of these values on the door to the staff lounge, in annual reports, and within advertised job descriptions is the trend.

Some staff members place a high value on honesty and integrity, while others lower the bar of ethical behavior. Some strive to fulfill the purpose of their organization and their unit's role, while others never grasp the central purpose of a library. Some recognize the benefits of lifelong learning and strive to be their best in the workplace—and draw out the best in their colleagues—while others are stuck in a rut and focus on what's wrong, no matter what the library's core values state.

"Through my words, actions, and decisions, I convey library goals and my 'whys' to senior coordinators, who in turn convey these to front-line staff. I check in for progress reports and to see how I can support my team's work; however, I mainly stay out of the way and let the 'magic' happen," says Carrie Plymire, Calvert (MD) Library director and Public Library Association board member. If you are a leader who values honesty, understands the purpose of a library, and sparks curiosity in yourself and others, your team will follow suit. They will become courageous collaborators on a mission to fulfill the organization's purpose. Leaders can pose questions—the right questions—in order to get people to think things through and get them on the same page with the director:

- A successful library is one in pursuit of an identity. What is the real goal—and glory—of my library? How can the library enlighten humanity?
- What is the role of my unit within the larger organization?
- What is the role of my position? What purpose does it serve?
- What good can I do today? What good have I done today? What harm might be done today? How might I defuse it and transform it?
- How can I approach each situation with optimism and thoughtfulness?
- Is pondering this statement an "a-ha" moment for me: where I focus my attention, energy will follow?
- How can I bring out the best in someone's character in order to better serve my organization and community? How can I create a robust liaison with colleagues in other departments or units within my organization—and with people in the community my library serves?
- How can I enrich my work with humor, cheerfulness, and harmony?

Nina Lindsay, the Oakland (CA) Public Library children's services coordinator and president (2017–18) of the Association for Library Service to Children, says, "The library offers a remarkable opportunity to bring a bit of goodwill to each person we serve, no matter what their need, mood, or level of optimism

FIGURE 8.3

Executive Library Director Leah Hamilton demonstrates fun physics by hosting a watermelon exploding activity.

Photo: Courtesy of Phelps (NY) Library and STEAM Lab Makerspace

or lack thereof." If your organization considers "love of learning" to be a core value, each employee should embrace the idea of learning for him or herself and for others. Are we learning the right things and applying them in our daily work? How can we cultivate goodwill during our interactions with customers and colleagues?

"The concept of being open to learning—anywhere, anytime—is elegantly simple, and suggests that learners across all developmental periods, from infancy to adulthood, gain knowledge and skills in multiple places and across all hours of the day," says Margaret Caspe of the Global Family Research Project.[7] Expanding this concept of developing a passion for learning—the right kind of learning—results in library leaders and staffers cultivating their own self-initiated learning.

But what about the wrong kind of learning—learning to be angry, learning to resent something you disagree with, or learning to be a sloppy thinker? Taking things out of context, making them negative, and overreacting are examples of misguided learning. Worrying, gossiping, and pettiness can keep us distracted from the larger picture. The right kind of learning can be seen when we bolster our curiosity, revise our beliefs when we understand our shortcomings, and integrate new insights into who we are and how we can better fulfill the director's vision. It's an ongoing process of unlearning and learning.

A key to getting staff on the right page is "unlearning." As a leader, do you ask questions as a way to examine what needs unlearning in your library?

- As you hire new people, do you teach them as soon as they start how to unlearn any bad personal habits of thinking negatively and reacting badly to colleagues and to customers?
- Do supervisors send a signal or subtle pressure to new staff *not* to shake things up and to go along in order to get along?
- How do new and experienced staff members unlearn in order to make productive decisions, not foolish ones?
- Can you admit limitations and examine organizational assumptions?
- Can you set right priorities and pace yourself in order to avoid burnout?
- What techniques do you employ to adjust your emotions in order to be calm and cooperative in each situation?
- Do you or others tend to think in black-and-white terms or default to the "us vs. them" syndrome?
- Do you research and gather enough information and evidence to explore a situation thoroughly? Do you delve deeply into a topic in order to discover the best solution, instead of defaulting to the first quick fix?
- Do you have a hard time thinking about your library in an ideal way?

Abraham Lincoln was not just an expert on learning—he called himself "a learner always"—but perfected the ability to avoid the comfort-of-the-herd type of thinking in his work. He mastered how to unlearn—and discern—as each case presented itself. "It is very common in this country to find great facility of expression and less common to find great lucidity of thought. The combination of the two in one person is very uncommon; but whenever you do find it, you have a great man," Lincoln told the English journalist Edward Dicey.[8] Lincoln teaches us how to manage opportunities and how to get along with people who may despise us.

In order to convey library purpose, strong central leadership is required, bringing out the best in individuals and molding a high-performing team. A director must first think through the big picture and then rally staff to become an effective unit. Otherwise, staff members will not be on the right page and the team can fall apart.

If anyone working in a library believes they know better than customers—or *certain* customers—they are probably on the wrong page. There may be thousands of books and millions of pages in the stacks. However, a tenth-grade-level calculus page should not be in a preschool picture book, nor should an angry page be in a library science book about customer service. Why turn to the wrong page? Let's get on the same page *carefully*. It must be the page of the director. The director's role is to lead, guide, and embody the library's purpose.

Let's think things through completely and celebrate the idea of working together with all customers. It doesn't matter whether library staffers arrive at work happy or grumpy on any particular day; if they stay on the same page as the director—to enlighten humanity through information, programs, books, and services—they will carry a community forward and help it thrive! No matter how many books may be in your library, it's still important to get all staff on the same page of the director.

NOTES

1. Monticello.org, https://www.monticello.org/site/research-and-collections/i-never -considered-difference-opinion-politicsquotation.
2. WinstonChurchill.org, https://www.winstonchurchill.org/?s=keep+calm.
3. WinstonChurchill.org, https://www.winstonchurchill.org/the-life-of-churchill/life/ churchill-leader-and-statesman.
4. Adapted from Dorothy Stoltz et al., *Inspired Collaboration: Ideas for Discovering and Applying Your Potential* (Chicago: American Library Association, 2016), 75–76.
5. Carl Sandburg, *Abraham Lincoln: The War Years*, vol. 1 (New York: Harcourt, Brace & World, 1939), 636.
6. Walt Whitman, *The Complete Prose Works*, available online at fullbooks.com, www.fullbooks.com/Complete-Prose-Works1.html.
7. Christine Patton and Margaret Caspe, *Finding Time Together: Families, Schools, and Communities Supporting Anywhere, Anytime Learning* (Harvard Family Research Project publication, 2014), 2.
8. Don E. Fehrenbacher and Virginia Fehrenbacher, eds., *Recollected Words of Abraham Lincoln* (Stanford, CA: Stanford University Press, 1996), 139.

Nine

FINDING TREASURES IN YOUR STACKS

Other men say wise things as well as he; only they say a good many foolish things, and do not know when they have spoken wisely.

RALPH WALDO EMERSON, FROM THE ESSAY "SHAKESPEARE; OR, THE POET"

Why should communities bother with libraries? As librarians, it's our job to know the answer to this question. Libraries can be proud of a rich heritage: creating an atmosphere in which to read and relish great writers and thinkers. Library professionals can usually find everything they need to help a community thrive in their own collections. As a result, librarians can answer the question of why communities should bother with libraries, which may be posed by funders as well as community members, by dipping into the books in the stacks, virtually and physically. Librarians come and go, but *libraries can remain anchored in their community by collecting, cherishing, and promoting books, authors, and ideas that stand the test of time.* Although popular, escapist reading has its value for all of us, the greatest treasures in a library often sit unused on the bookshelf.

One of the most useful gems is the works of William Shakespeare. Shakespearean dramas are not just a bunch of dusty pages in an old tome; there is a living presence in his plays. Shakespeare symbolizes great writing par excellence and should be at the heart of every library. Such writings, in fact, are our lifeblood. They help libraries develop a culture where each person is responsible for his or her own learning and where risk-taking is valued. Does your library celebrate the genius of Shakespeare or hide it?

Libraries, museums, and other community settings were part of the American Library Association and the Folger Shakespeare Library's traveling exhibition in 2016 called *The Wonder of Will: 400 Years of Shakespeare*. The centerpiece of the celebration was the First Folio, the 1623 collection of Shakespeare's plays in one volume. Libraries can be inspired by Henry and Emily Folger's love of Shakespeare, their quest to collect Shakespeare, and the establishment of their library in 1932 to do good work. The Folger Library, located in Washington, DC, is a cultural treasure and a national anchor; each main library and local branch should likewise be a satellite anchor shining the light of wisdom through its community. *This above all—to thine own self be true, and it must follow, as night follows day, thou canst not then be false to anyone.* Every library can use great literature to focus its collection, programs, and services in a way that acts as its neighborhood's treasure.

FIGURE 9.1

The first folio (1623) is the first published collection of William Shakespeare's plays. Scholars consider it to be one of the most influential books ever published in the English language. STC 22273 Fo.1 no.68 [Works. 1623] *Mr. William Shakespeares comedies, histories, & tragedies : published according to the true originall copies.* leaf ℗A1 verso (To the Reader) || leaf ℗A1+1 recto (title page).

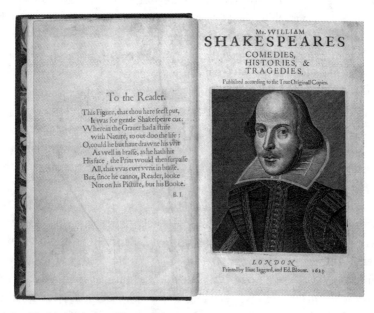

By permission of the Folger Shakespeare Library

FIGURE 9.2

The San Diego Public Library created a message board for patrons to share how Shakespeare's words are still relevant today. The exhibit, *The Old Globe with San Diego Public Library*, June 4, 2016–July 7, 2016, was part of the ALA/Folger traveling exhibition, *The Wonder of Will: 400 Years of Shakespeare*.

Photo: D. Stoltz

The Boston Public Library holds one of the largest and most comprehensive collections of Shakespeare publications in a public institution, including rare editions of plays like *Hamlet* and *The Merchant of Venice*. To highlight its impressive collection, the library featured *All the City's a Stage: A Season of Shakespeare* with exhibits, author talks, lectures, theatrical performances, book clubs, film screenings, youth programs, and workshops. Many other libraries with modest collections, such as the Oxford School Shakespeare paperback series, celebrated Shakespeare in 2016 as well. Library staffers, for example, at the Washington County (MD) Free Library held Shakespeare readings along with activities for children.

The Philadelphia Free Library features numerous special collections, such as manuscript letters of presidents of the United States dating from 1780, three John Keats first editions, and the original manuscript of Beatrix Potter's *The Tailor of Gloucester*. Clara Clemens donated several items from her father's estate to the Detroit Public Library to create a Samuel Clemens (Mark Twain) Collection, which includes the original manuscript of the unfinished story *Huck Finn and Tom Sawyer among the Indians*. A beautifully illustrated early edition of James Audubon's *Birds of North America* can be viewed in the Northwest Room Fuller collection at the Spokane (WA) Public Library. The Enoch Pratt Free Library's special collections include the original manuscripts of Edgar Allan Poe's poems "To Elizabeth" and "The Bells."

"The general public feels that it has a stake in the public library and, therefore, approaches its special collections without hesitation,"[1] wrote Ellen Shaffer, a special collections librarian, in 1957. This statement is as relevant today as it was sixty years ago. Examining original editions and manuscripts published or produced during the time of the author gives the reader a direct connection to the author's ideas. "Although much of our collection is digitized and widely used, researchers appreciate the opportunity to spend a couple of hours reading an original manuscript before their project goes to print," said Betsy Walsh, former head of reader services at the Folger Shakespeare Library.

However, not all libraries can collect special editions. We can collect, promote, and delight in reading modern paperback versions of *The Merchant of Venice*, or *The Complete Tales & Poems of Edgar Allan Poe*, or *Nature* by Ralph Waldo Emerson. The overarching goal is to plant the seed of inspiration from great thinkers by making their books available for free—in hardcover, paperback, or e-book versions—in libraries. We can create opportunities for discussion through programming and encourage people of all ages to ponder how great writers' ideas can help bring communities together.

BROWSE, EXPLORE, AND DISCOVER

Let's strengthen the role of the library as a place to browse, explore, and discover ideas that can motivate, inspire, and stimulate our communities to be their best—economically, educationally, and culturally. Why should Shakespeare and other dead white men be part of that role?

Great writers and thinkers, like Shakespeare, who have helped enlighten human-ity have stood the test of time. Thomas Jefferson noted that a "lively and lasting sense of filial duty is more effectually impressed on the mind of a son or daughter by reading *King Lear*, than by all the volumes of ethics and divinity that ever were written."[2] John Adams saluted Shakespeare as "that great Master of every Affection of the Heart and every sentiment of the Mind as well as all the Powers of Expression."[3]

Elizabeth Barrett Browning put it thus:

> There Shakespeare, on whose forehead climb
> The crowns o' the world; oh, eyes sublime
> With tears and laughter for all time

Ben Jonson wrote in the preface of the First Folio,

> Soule of the Age!
> The applause! delight! The wonder of our stage!

During Shakespeare's lifetime (1564–1616) society was rapidly changing in ways that helped humanity grow. European merchants ventured across the oceans to find quicker ways to commercial markets of the "Far East" in the early seventeenth century. England and Europe wanted to increase commerce and trade, develop cultural inspiration, and uplift their societies. In the midst of their explorations they discovered the continent of North America. Worldwide undercurrents for the independence and freedom of "peasants," "lower classes," "women," and "slaves" were emerging, leading to the American Revolutionary War and the Civil War in the United States.

"The Muses would speak with Shakespeare's fine filed phrase if they would speak English,"[4] reflected Francis Meres in 1598. This observation suggests that Shakespeare not only helped mold the English language from a stilted form of communication to a dynamic form of expression, but he also *tapped life's inspiration for creativity, redemption, and wisdom.* The growing force of freedom in Shakespeare's time—from peasant and landlord-run communities to a slow but steadily growing working and middle class—was demonstrated through his plays and sonnets. First, the characters in his works were often more complex, alive, and psychologically interesting than the characterizations of previous playwrights. Second, Shakespeare helped transform the

Era	Approximate Time Period	Example: The Lord's Prayer
Old English The time of the Beowulf poet	450–1066	Fæder ure þu þe eart on heofonum; Si þin nama gehalgod to becume þin rice gewurþe ðin willa on eorðan swa swa on heofonum.
Middle English The time of Chaucer	1066–1450	Oure fadir that art in heuenes, halewid be thi name; thi kyndoom come to; be thi wille don in erthe as in heuene.
Early Modern English The time of Shakespeare	1450–1690	Our father which art in heauen, hallowed be thy name. Thy kingdome come. Thy will be done, in earth, as it is in heauen.
Modern English The time of Alexander Pope	1690–1900	Our Father, who art in heaven, Hallowed be thy Name. Thy kingdom come. Thy will be done, On earth as it is in heaven.
Today's English	1900–Present	Our Father, who art in heaven, hallowed be your name. Your kingdom come. Your will be done, on earth as it is in heaven.

English language. There is still much to be learned from Shakespeare, despite the grumblings of high school students (but not librarians, we hope) about his stilted and old-fashioned language. The chart on the preceding page illustrates the progression of written and spoken language from Old English to our modern English.[5]

Going back to the times of the *Beowulf* poet and Chaucer with wording such as "faeder ure" and "oure fadir" may be going back too far to create a popular library program for anyone other than the occasional English literature enthusiast. However, in going back to Shakespeare, we find easy access to the English language as a living, growing phenomenon. Shakespeare's plays offer a treasure trove for understanding how people behave, think, and redeem themselves using the beauty of language and the force of life. For example:

Sweetest nut hath sourest rind; Such a nut is Rosalind

As You Like It, Act III, Scene II

For there is nothing either good or bad, but thinking makes it so.

The Tragedy of Hamlet, Act II, Scene II

God be wi' you: let's meet as little as we can. (Jacques)
I do desire we may be better strangers. (Orlando)

As You Like It, Act III, Scene I

The quality of mercy is not strained.
It droppeth as the gentle rain from heaven
Upon the place beneath. It is twice blest:
It blesseth him that gives and him that takes.

The Merchant of Venice, Act 4, Scene 1

My answer is like a barber's chair that fits all buttocks, the pin-buttock, the quatch-buttock, the brawn-buttock, or any buttock.

All's Well that Ends Well, Act III, Scene II

You, minion, are too saucy.

Two Gentlemen of Verona, Act I, Scene II

In addition, Shakespeare's poetic works, full of characterization, language, plot, and action, helped to expand the expectations of popular theater, raised its status, and boosted its acceptability as a source of inspiration and wisdom, as well as a form of entertainment. Jefferson reminds us that the plays help "fix us in the principles and practices of virtue"[6] and in the aversion of vice.

In 1831 Alexis de Tocqueville, a French political writer, traveled in the United States, observing, "There is hardly a pioneer's hut which does not contain a few odd volumes of Shakespeare."[7] De Tocqueville wrote in his two-part publication, *Democracy in America*, that he read *Henry V* for the first time in a log cabin during his brief American tour.

WHY OFFER REGULAR LIBRARY PROGRAMMING ON GREAT LITERATURE?

Library staffers can dust off Shakespeare's works and spread curiosity and enthusiasm for great literature. A wondrous example of how a library connects people to Shakespeare is at the New York Public Library. Frank Collerius, manager of the Jefferson Market (Greenwich Village) Library, called Cecilia Rubino, asking, "I heard you teach Shakespeare at the New School; can you do something *at the library?*"

Through an informal word-of-mouth promotion, a large audience of all ages and socioeconomic backgrounds gathered each week at the Jefferson Market Library. Rubino was amazed at the public response to her four-week lecture series on Shakespeare. The initial series, which focused on Shakespeare in memory, love, and forgiveness, was followed by her popular eight-week seminar at Jefferson Market Library called "Acting Shakespeare for Seniors." A new version of the Shakespeare for Seniors course was offered in spring 2017 at the Thompkins Square Library and focused on *Midsummer Night's Dream* and *Julius Caesar*, the two plays that were performed at the Public Theater's free Shakespeare in the Park over the summer. Rubino said, "We discovered that many older adults memorized Shakespeare growing up as part of their school experience. They were excited not only to recite passages from the plays and sonnets, but were eager to share why the words were important for them."

In following up with interviews of participants for a documentary film project—in production as of this writing called *Remembering Shakespeare*—Rubino is capturing how Shakespeare can provide insights into our lives. "When young people ask 'what does a 400-year-old dead white guy have to do with me?' I say it's because Shakespeare poses questions about life to help us think deeply about its purpose and meaning," explains Rubino. It might also have something to do with our children finding Shakespeare preserved by libraries, of course.

Libraries can collaborate with schools, theaters, museums, or any Shakespeare appreciator to read, recite, memorize, act out, sing, and otherwise promote "the Bard" and thus help transform and invigorate our communities. The eagerness of people of all ages, education levels, and backgrounds to respond to the genius of Shakespeare may be surprising.

During the First Folio national tour in 2016 sponsored by the ALA and Folger Library, many host sites shared the history of their community's connection with Shakespeare. The Lake County Discovery Museum in Illinois featured one of its artifacts—Marlon Brando's Mark Antony costume from the 1953 film *Julius Caesar*. Cheyenne, Wyoming, boasted that from the early nineteenth century when the trapper, scout, and "mountain man" Jim Bridger, with no formal education, brought his love of Shakespeare to Cheyenne, Shakespeare has been an integral part of its culture.

FIGURE 9.3

Acting Shakespeare seminar, New York Public Library.

Photo: Peter Lucas

FIGURE 9.4

Marlon Brando's Mark Antony costume from the 1953 film *Julius Caesar.*

Photo: Courtesy of Lake County (IL) Discovery Museum

FIGURE 9.5

"We've provided the props and lines, the rest is up to you!" Prop Drop box in the exhibition hall at the Folger Shakespeare Library.

Photo: D. Stoltz

TREASURES UNLIMITED

Libraries can reinforce the efforts of schools and families to bring out the best in their children. Experiential learning is worthwhile in libraries through "makerspace" activities and STEM (science, technology, engineering, and math) programming. Offering Shakespeare and other great writers and thinkers through books and programs is not only important; it is a noble *and* realistic goal for any library. This can help individuals develop discernment skills and enhance inspired learning for all ages.

Another great author who ought to be highlighted in libraries is Alexander Pope, an eighteenth-century English poet. Thomas Jefferson told John Bernard, a famous British actor, that Shakespeare, as well as Alexander Pope, "gave him the perfection of imagination and judgment, both displaying more knowledge of the human heart—the true province of poetry—than he could find elsewhere."[8] Pope is the second most-cited writer appearing in the *Oxford Dictionary of Quotations* after Shakespeare. Do you recognize these Pope quotes?

A little learning is a dangerous thing;
Drink deep, or taste not the Pierian spring.
Fools rush in where angels fear to tread.
To be angry is to revenge the faults of others on ourselves.
Hope springs eternal in the human breast:
Man never is, but always to be blest.
Blessed is the man who expects nothing,
    for he shall never be disappointed was the ninth beatitude.
Teach me to feel another's woe, to hide the fault I see,
    that mercy I to others show, that mercy show to me.
Trust not yourself, but your defects to know,
    make use of every friend and every foe.
Tis but a part we see, and not a whole.

In the realm of science, libraries can promote Nikola Tesla's works and life. Tesla was an electrical engineer, physicist, and futurist whose inventions in the early twentieth century set the stage for many technological breakthroughs, including alternating current (AC) electricity and wireless communication. Tesla described his creative thinking as a long process of thinking about an idea for months or years at a time without deliberate concentration, carefully choosing the best solutions to investigate, and then intentionally downloading the best answer. "The whole idea is worked out mentally. In my mind I change the construction, make improvements, and even operate the device. Without ever having drawn a sketch I can give measurements of all parts to workmen, and when completed all these parts will fit, just as certainly as though I had made the actual drawings," said Tesla.[9]

Sir Francis Bacon, an English philosopher, statesman, scientist, author, and contemporary of Shakespeare, was devoted to discovering truth and pioneered the scientific method. "No pleasure is comparable to the standing upon the vantage ground of truth (a hill not to be commanded, and where the air is always clear and serene), and to see the errors, and wanderings, and mists, and tempests, in the vale below; so always that this prospect be with pity, and not with swelling, or pride,"[10] wrote Bacon.

Why is it valuable to browse and explore timeless treasures in our collections? As J. R. R. Tolkien wrote, "All that is gold does not glitter."[11] It is common to ignore authors who have been around a long time and may not be in vogue. By discovering our treasures in the stacks, it forces us to think about the bigger picture and stop using a narrow focus that excludes things, ideas, and authors that are too good to miss!

Bringing Shakespeare, Bacon, Emerson, Pope, Tesla, and others off the library shelf and into the heart of the community can serve as a reminder of the purpose of a library: to stimulate and enlighten society—and it is also a reminder to support the library. This role—to enlighten humanity through books, programs, and services—involves more than just literacy and reading: it reaches into the core of how a library can help transform a community by inspiring its members to bring out the best in themselves and each other. It's where "the rubber meets the road" in activating how a library can enrich life. Libraries can offer programs that feature great literature not just once or twice a year, but on a regular, consistent, and joyful basis.

Where else in the community can this role be manifested as magnificently as at the library? Nowhere! Who other than librarians have all the right skills, resources, and dedication to "do good" in the community through great literature—as Benjamin Franklin might ask? No one! How else to better improve the library and increase your rapport with the community? With a nod to Cole Porter:

> Funders today in society
> Go for classical poetry
> So to win their hearts you must quote with ease
> Aeschylus and Euripides
> But the poet of them all
> Who will start 'em simply ravin'
> Is the poet people call
> The Bard of Stratford-on-Avon
> Brush up your Shakespeare
> Start quoting him now
> Brush up your Shakespeare
> And the funders you will wow!

NOTES

1. Ellen Shaffer, "The Place of Rare Books in the Public Library," *Library Trends* 5, no. 4 (Spring 1957).

2. Thomas Jefferson to Robert Skipwith, August 3, 1771, "Thomas Jefferson Encyclopedia," Thomas Jefferson Monticello website, https://www.monticello.org/site/research -and-collections/william-shakespeare.

3. Peter R. Boller, Jr., "The American Presidents and Shakespeare," *White House History*, no. 30 (Fall 2011): 4–5, https://www.whitehousehistory.org/the-american-presidents -and-shakespeare.

4. Francis Meres, *Palladis Tamia, Wits Treasury* (London: Printed by P. Short for Cuthbert Burbie, 1598), www.bartleby.com/359/31.html.

5. Adapted from J. M. Pressley and the Shakespeare Resource Center, www.bardweb.net/ language.html.

6. Boller, "The American Presidents and Shakespeare," 13, https://www.whitehousehistory .org/the-american-presidents-and-shakespeare.

7. Alexis de Tocqueville, *Democracy in America*, vol. 2: *Influence of Democracy on Progress of Opinion in the United States*, trans. Henry Reeve, Gutenberg Project (2006); first edition, *De la démocratie en Amérique* (London: Saunders and Otley, 1835–40).

8. Boller, "The American Presidents and Shakespeare," 10, https://www.whitehousehistory .org/the-american-presidents-and-shakespeare.

9. John J. O'Neill, *Prodigal Genius: The Life of Nikola Tesla* (Kempton, IL: Adventures Unlimited, 2008), 257.

10. Francis Bacon, "Of Truth" (1625), in *Essays or Counsels, Moral and Civil*, http://fly .hiwaay.net/~paul/bacon/essays/truth.html.

11. J. R. R. Tolkien, *The Fellowship of the Ring*, chap. 10.

PART IV
ACTIVATE CREATIVITY!

Ten

THE ENTREPRENEURIAL SPIRIT

The rising tide lifts all boats.

JOHN F. KENNEDY, QUOTING AN OLD NEW ENGLAND SAYING

Just as a Shakespearean play poses questions about the meaning of life and can help refresh our minds, we need to ask questions in ways that encourage those working in libraries to activate creative thinking in all who use the library. While a library that offers excellent customer service experiences is more likely to be funded by its community, an even higher level of reciprocity also occurs between a library and its community. A library cannot be creative unless the community is creative. And a community is more likely to transcend traditional ideas, patterns, and relationships if the library plants seeds of innovation and creative change.

Customer engagement means encouraging individuals to display helpfulness, respect, integrity, accountability, and proactive thinking—in their domestic, work, and community responsibilities. Customer enrichment means helping individuals play their part and discover ideas, philosophies, and methods that will carry them to greater accomplishments in their area of life, such as education, science, government, business, health care, and the arts. The library director and staffers have a rich opportunity to inspire people. Libraries can offer not only activities, collaborative work spaces, and books, but also help people refresh their minds. *The library can be a magnet for people to develop active minds.* In this way, a library can energize the community—and society—to remake itself. This level of creative thinking and doing is the ultimate outreach!

Questions for today's librarian might begin with:

- How can you help your organization succeed? What does success mean?
- How can you best serve your community in ways that help "all boats rise"?
- What are you learning from your community? Who can you turn to for inspiration?
- Why should librarians—who often work in nonprofit or government-affiliated organizations—examine private sector entrepreneurship?
- What is the essence of true entrepreneurship? How can this essence be applied by organizations in the public sector, such as libraries?

Since each library serves a community with different points of need, accomplishments will differ from library to library. However, the basis of success is the same no matter what the community. A library has its best chance for success when everyone in the organization stays focused on its primary purpose—finding ways to enlighten humanity. *A thriving library helps a community stay well-motivated to think creatively and proactively during good times as well as when facing complex challenges.*

By looking up the language roots associated with the words "success" and "purpose," a helpful pattern of understanding emerges. The Old English word *spaden* means "to succeed." The Proto-Indo European *spo-ti* means "to thrive." From the fifteenth and sixteenth centuries, the phrases "on purpose" and "of purpose" imply *by design*. The skills needed to activate our best thinking and produce favorable outcomes in life are part of the human design. The right use of creative energy stimulates success and helps all of us learn, transform, and thrive.

People who become enduring successes have the ability to dedicate a major portion of their thoughts and actions to the purpose of their field. "Enlightening humanity" is a shared purpose among the arts, libraries, and schools. Personal causes are not the same as purpose. A personal cause has a narrow function. A purpose, by contrast, is sufficiently abstract to trigger intelligent risk-taking and avoid a limited focus. It helps us spark curiosity and discover solutions not initially envisioned. It prevents an outstanding project from sinking down into trifling details. Purpose is broad, timeless, and an inspiration to people after hundreds of years.

FIGURE 10.1

Collaborative work spaces in libraries allow people to make creative connections with each other.

Photo: Courtesy of Steelcase Education

What purpose do you serve in your position or role for the library? By thinking in terms of the purpose of a library—a top-down approach—you are more likely to understand and be effective in your role. Take a moment or two to think about how your role supports the library's purpose of enlightening humanity.

"If your inspiration is simply cash or 'an opening in the market,' you're likely to turn back at the first sign of hardship. If your inspiration is close to your heart, you won't stop until you get there,"[1] says Ajay Yadav, founder and CEO at Roomi. Likewise for librarians, if our inspiration is simply to increase our circulation or attendance statistics, we are unlikely to succeed in the long term.

Andrew Carnegie stayed focused on what could be done in a huge company to benefit humanity and then what could be done with excess money to enlighten humanity. "I took it to bed with me at night, and I took it to work with me in the morning. My definite purpose became more than a mere wish; it became my burning desire!" said Carnegie. He added, "My job is to keep my employees inspired with a desire to do the finest possible job . . . My major purpose in life is the development of people."[2] Carnegie's focus on purpose helped transform the steel industry's capability to build stronger steel for better and safer buildings, railroads, and bridges. It benefited humanity's ability to grow and thrive in commerce, business, and transportation. Carnegie's focus on enlightening humanity through public libraries has helped thousands and thousands of individuals to thrive.

A library's culture, budget, and level of staffing help determine what it can and cannot do. A specific formula that will guarantee success does not exist. However, focusing on the library's purpose—to enlighten humanity—will help employees create and sustain success. The talent and creativity of staff members are our greatest resource for ongoing success. Insights into defining and achieving success from great thinkers include:

Success is walking from failure to failure with
no loss of enthusiasm.
—Winston Churchill

Try not to become a person of success,
but rather try to become a person of value.
—Albert Einstein

What seems to us as bitter trials are often blessings in disguise.
—Oscar Wilde

The will to win, the desire to succeed, the urge to reach your full
potential . . . these are the keys that will unlock the door
to personal excellence.
—Confucius

FIGURE 10.2

Build-a-bat-house activity engages families to stimulate thinking, practice patience, and acquire new skills.

Photo: Courtesy of Cohocton (NY) Public Library

Character cannot be developed in ease and quiet.
Only through experience of trial and effort can the soul be
strengthened, ambition inspired, and success achieved.

—Helen Keller

Courage is resistance to fear, mastery of fear—not absence of fear.

—Mark Twain

Don't judge each day by the harvest you reap
but by the seeds you plant.

—Robert Louis Stevenson

What the mind can conceive, it can achieve.

—Andrew Carnegie

A NEW WAY TO VIEW THE LIBRARY'S ROLE

"Bertie is in the toils of an adventuress," screamed his mother in the 1911 short story "Shock Tactics" by the English writer H. H. Munro, aka Saki.[3] When it comes to raising her nineteen-year-old son, Mrs. Heasant is in the habit of controlling Bertie, and she freely reads his correspondence as soon as the mail arrives. One day this backfires. As a hoax, his friend, Clovis, sends a letter to Bertie from a fictitious "Clotilde," knowing that Mrs. Heasant will read it. "Clotilde" entangles Bertie in plotting the theft of jewels and promoting chicanery. Mrs. Heasant is fooled until a letter arrives in the final evening post. Clovis writes as himself explaining the spoof and his intent to give anyone who might open the previous letter "something exciting to read." Bertie's mother admits defeat in order to avoid embarrassment and releases her son to make his own decisions in life.

Witty, insightful, and courageous, H. H. Munro was an adventurer who was willing to take risks. He served in the British colonial Burmese military police until ill health brought him back to England, where he became a journalist and short-story writer challenging Edwardian society.

How does the spirit of adventure translate into making libraries relevant? What does it mean to act with a keen sense of intelligent adventure—but not to make impetuous or ill-considered decisions? The long-term renovation of a branch gave the DC Public Library the opportunity to rethink how to engage people throughout Washington, DC, who were not current library users. By creating a temporary, three-year outreach department, the DC Public Library is tapping that sense of adventure.

Library staffers who take the time to think things through find effective means to attain desirable results. Can librarians be intelligently adventurous and willing to risk everything to enlighten humanity? Absolutely! Nikola Tesla (1856–1943), the brilliant electrical engineer, entrepreneur, and inventor, is an outstanding demonstration of what is possible when everything is risked.

As a boy Tesla was constantly experimenting and received "flashes" of insight about the potential of how things work. He created a smooth-disk water wheel which later resurfaced in his invention of a smooth-disk turbine. He helped a fire company solve a problem with its new pumping apparatus and at age seven became a local hero. He developed his original methods of power production by designing and successfully operating a bug-power motor. In an instant Tesla had a flash of understanding as a young adult about the fundamentals of electricity, and he spent a lifetime trying to express all that he learned. When Tesla was ten or eleven years old he made up his mind to start his work at three o'clock in the morning and "continue until eleven o'clock at night, no Sundays or holidays excepted." He said, "I waded through books of several libraries . . . choosing my subjects as I liked."[4] This started a lifelong routine of extraordinary dedication to a cause for the greater good.

Tesla did not speak of his own accomplishments, but instead spoke of the value of his inventions to the world. For example, he wrote in 1919, "With the first 'World-System' power plant it will be practical to attain electrical activities up to ten million horsepower and it is designed to serve for as many technical achievements as are possible without due expense."[5]

Tesla was a discoverer of principles that continue to be explored today: electric power, motors, radio, radar, fluorescent and neon lighting, high-frequency currents, wireless capability, and robotics. Hundreds of Tesla's insights are still unused. Tesla risked everything to show what could be done. Presenting his ideas to the world was more important to him than agreeing

FIGURE 10.3

Nikola Tesla, 1900

Photo: Library of Congress.
LC-B2- 1026-9 [P&P] Repository.
Library of Congress Prints and
Photographs Division Washington, D.C.

to a contract with a company that would hinder his creativity. He sold patents to others on their own terms so he could get on with the work at hand. He died without much money compared to what he could have made, but he enriched humanity for many years to come.

The *New York Sun* wrote in an editorial after Tesla's death in 1943: "[Tesla] . . . was seeing a glimpse into that confused and mysterious frontier which divides the known and the unknown . . . [and] was trying with superb intelligence to find the answers. His guesses were right so often that he would be frightening. Probably we shall appreciate him better a few million years from now."[6]

PUBLIC LIBRARY ENTREPRENEURSHIP

Should library staffers become workaholics? No. Can librarians dedicate themselves to taking time to think things through completely and joyfully? Yes! The key is tapping the essence of the entrepreneurial spirit and bringing it into the library organization and infusing it into library morale. True entrepreneurs tend to be good at perceiving new opportunities, and they embrace a risk-taking attitude that makes them more likely to exploit those opportunities. Most nonprofit and government-affiliated libraries have people—a library board or elected officials—to say "You can't do this or that." Therefore, librarians cannot be true entrepreneurs, but we can catch the spirit of entrepreneurship and encourage people to become entrepreneurs. Is there a Nikola Tesla in your community? Is there a budding entrepreneur who will wade through books and learn intensively at your library in order to find the inspiration he or she will need? How will you know?

Public sector entrepreneurship requires curiosity about the best within ourselves and others, and the right attitude about being adventurous—using intelligence and courage, and having the willingness to explore and apply new perspectives.

Libraries can breathe life into communities by encouraging intelligent risk-taking. The public sector entrepreneurial spirit can be defined as inner vitality and the ability to

- dedicate a large chunk of time day in and day out to enlightening humanity
- focus the mind to think creatively and completely
- be willing to risk everything for the greater good

- sustain oneself for long periods without frequent encouragement and praise
- plant seeds that will grow into private sector entrepreneurship
- recognize the potential for long-term impact without always seeing immediate, tangible results.

Tesla found inspiration by reading books in libraries during his youth in the 1860s and 1870s. It took another ten to twenty years before that inspiration manifested itself in phenomenal productivity as an adult. It took an additional twenty or more years for worldwide recognition of his inventiveness. Only in 2003, sixty years after his death, was an electric car and a company named after him. Can libraries tap that kind of entrepreneurial spirit without expecting immediate results? Can we build a bridge to the community to help people thrive despite not seeing short-term results? Can we recognize and pursue opportunities for long-term results? Can we approach our work as planting seeds, while knowing that not all outcomes will be measured at the end of a strategic plan?

Of course, private sector entrepreneurs and companies need to make a profit in order to stay in business. However, their overarching purpose is the business at hand, such as producing a product to help humanity in some way. Their purpose is not to focus on making money per se. Libraries need funding streams in order to serve the community. But their purpose is the enlightenment of humanity, not a focus on increasing the circulation of books.

In virtually every community librarians can plant seeds to help people make connections and tap the entrepreneurial spirit. Libraries can offer high-tech and low-tech activities and dedicate resources and spaces for individual and group collaboration to explore, learn, and create. "We've learned how offering technology training and access to a mini-laser engraver can inspire a 22-year-old college dropout to start his own wedding glass engraving business," says Felton Thomas, director of the Cleveland (OH) Public Library and president of the Public Library Association (2016–2017).

Many libraries, as another example, feature well-attended author programs. Although one function of these programs may be to demonstrate participation numbers or raise funds to help sustain financial support from the community, the goal is to have meaningful presentations and discussions that can uplift and inspire residents. Can these events connect people to

FIGURE 10.4

A touch-screen wall offers an interactive way for patrons to learn more about exhibits and collection highlights.

Photo: Courtesy of Cleveland Public Digital Library

FIGURE 10.5

Can you infuse public sector entrepreneurial spirit into your library staff by hosting author events? Audience members holding up their copies of the book at an author event for a group photo.

Photo: Courtesy of Carroll County (MD) Public Library

the entrepreneurial spirit so that they start their own business adventure? Enriching conversations and insights from fiction and nonfiction authors can be helpful. Risk-taking can be inspired by great literature and fictional characters as well as historical figures, businesspeople, and anyone promoting the entrepreneurial spirit.

Taking authors outside the library walls, Jack McBride White, author of *In Carrie's Footprints: The Long Walk of Warren Dorsey*, and Warren Dorsey visited a retirement community. White wrote this powerful story about the life and times of Warren Gamaliel Dorsey. Dorsey, the grandson of a slave, succeeded in lifting himself out of an impoverished childhood to become a scientist, teacher, and school principal.

A well-attended author visit with a lively discussion is a simple illustration, but it is a perfect opportunity to plant seeds that will grow into the spirit of entrepreneurship. Library staff should dedicate their time, energy, and a risk-taking mentality to make these types of activities a success. The St. Paul (MN) Public Library risked bringing in five *New York Times* bestselling authors for an Opus & Olives fund-raiser in 2006. Such programs have nearly tripled participation over the years, netting $200,000 in 2016. A robust discussion occurring while a programming philosophy statement, guidelines, and checklists are being developed can help structure the thinking process to develop intelligent risks in planning programs.

Tapping the public-sector entrepreneurial spirit assists us in our role of helping people to refresh their intellect and cultivate an active mind. It involves developing an enlightened way for librarians to plan services and programs, design library spaces, and view and respond to the events of life in our communities. Being motivated by the entrepreneurial spirit, library staffers can upgrade their capability to open people's hearts and minds. They can apply that spirit in their efforts to plant seeds of inspiration and trigger the community to take risks. You may hear an elected official say to the librarian: "I don't know if we really know what a 'makerspace' is, but if you say it's good for our community, then we're all for it!" The goals are to devote our time, focus our minds, and be inclined to take risks in order to show what can be done.

"We connected with a virtual reality game developer, Hadar Silverman from Earthborn Interactive, to share his beta version of MageWorks with library customers in order to get feedback for his application. It also showcased how emerging technologies, such as virtual reality and 3-D printing,

FIGURE 10.6

A hundred people attended a presentation by Jack White (seated) and 95-year-old Warren Dorsey (standing) at a retirement community setting, sponsored by the library and the historical society.

Photo: Lisa Picker

FIGURE 10.7

Kahla Gubanich, Exploration Point makerspace librarian, leading a student to help a virtual reality game developer design an app.

Photo: Courtesy of Carroll County (MD) Public Library

are beginning to intersect and overlap," said Jen Bishop, the online services and emerging technology supervisor at the Carroll County Public Library. Shawn Harrison, the web designer for Carroll libraries, added, "Taking the time to figure out how to use cool technology has added to our workload, but it's worthwhile. The library is reaching thousands of people of all ages, giving them access to 3-D printing, virtual reality, and drones. The interest from the public is strong. The IT department wants to support staff and increase their skills and confidence in using the technologies."

Benjamin Franklin (1706–1790), inventor, entrepreneur, and printer, was able to "retire" from active business at age forty-two—though he remained fully engaged at the local, national, and international levels as an author, publisher, scientist, statesman, and diplomat. He demonstrated an array of entrepreneurial qualities ranging from being trustworthy and hard-working to taking intelligent risks and seeing the whole picture of a situation. Franklin had the knack for identifying and filling a gap, such as launching the popular *Philadelphische Zeitung*—the first newspaper printed in German in the American Colonies. He pioneered the mail order catalog as an inventive way to get rid of extra inventory. Franklin's constant pursuit of a better world did not always result in personal gain. However, "doing well by doing good" was a keystone to his success, both as an entrepreneur and as a human being.

How can a library embrace the entrepreneurial spirit and help "all boats rise"? What does it mean for a librarian to make an imprint on his or her community—and do well by doing good?

- Build a bridge to those enterprises in the community that are thriving—in order to learn from them and support them.
- Plant seeds by encouraging members of the community to embrace entrepreneurship—young and old alike.
- Kindle a symbolic bonfire of the mind by engaging customers with great thinkers, such as Nikola Tesla, Confucius, Benjamin Franklin, Elizabeth Barrett Browning, and Ralph Waldo Emerson.
- Spark curiosity within yourself and others in ways that produce creative solutions above anything thought possible, that is, *be open to the potential of solutions you cannot yet envision.*

FIGURE 10.8

Find your local treasures. The Frederick County (MD) Libraries' innovative "sidekicks" series reaches out to community members to present library programs. An example of an uplifting entrepreneurial story, Hoke made old world furniture in America with real hardwoods, no press board or fillers, and it is all hand-carved in the old world tradition. His grandson Steven Hoke was invited by the library to present the story of the Hoke family and their 1946 establishment of a premiere American furniture manufacturing company located in downtown Thurmont, Maryland. The program was presented in partnership with the Thurmont Historical Society.

By permission of Steven Hoke

NOTES

1. What Inspired You to Become an Entrepreneur? https://www.quora.com/What -inspired-you-to-be-an-entrepreneur.

2. Napoleon Hill, *Napoleon Hill's The Wisdom of Andrew Carnegie as Told to Napoleon Hill* (Wise, VA): Napoleon Hill Foundation, 2004), 8–9, 26.

3. EastoftheWeb, www.eastoftheweb.com/short-stories/UBooks/ShocTact.shtml.

4. Nikola Tesla, *My Inventions: The Autobiography of Nikola Tesla* (originally published in several installments for the magazine *Electrical Experimenter*, 1919; reprinted by Martino Publishing, 2011), 38.

5. Tesla, *My Inventions*, 69.

6. Marc J. Seifer, *The Life & Times of Nikola Tesla: Biography of a Genius* (New York: Citadel Press Books, 1998), 445.

Eleven

TAP INTO CREATIVE POTENTIAL

*Business people go down with their businesses because they like the
old way so well they cannot bring themselves to change.
One sees them all about—people who do not know that yesterday
is past, and who woke up this morning with their last year's ideas.*

HENRY FORD

What is creativity? Although creativity shines most brightly in the arts, creativity that champions new ideas is part of all areas of life and can be taught as a mental skill, based on learning to download the best ideas from abstract thinking. Creativity can be directly applied in libraries to write better grant proposals, develop common-sense customer service policies, incorporate flexibility in all that we do, find treasures in the stacks, design dynamic spaces, offer irresistible events, collaborate with partners in fresh ways, and respond appropriately and effectively to any problem, challenge, or barrier.

An illustration of creativity that transformed society in the United States is the building of the transcontinental railroad. It is easy to gloss over the importance of how railroads transformed life for the better in the nineteenth century. But what can libraries learn from the railway industry's growth, rejection, and rebirth as a vital American force?

Railroad leaders who focused on the big picture of improving society, as opposed to a narrow-minded fixation on profits, thrived in the long run. The enthusiasm for opening new frontiers, a pride in accomplishment, and fulfilling the public need for transportation kept influential thinkers focused on what was working and what could be done differently to be more effective. These factors helped keep their attention and energy centered on the growth of communities and the expansion of societal achievement. Making money was a way to stay in business and reinvest for continual improvement.

One of the library's major challenges is finding the right balance in serving everyone in the community. How can a library in a community with a homeless population best serve the homeless? How can such a library avoid appearing to be "a lobby of a social service agency" that could inhibit middle-class families from attending storytimes? The New York Public Library describes one function of its spaces as allowing people "to contemplate privately in public, among a world of ideas."[1] Yet, libraries are making room for play-and-learn centers and makerspace activities. How can libraries find the right balance between activity that encourages playful exploration and conversation on the one hand and opportunities for quiet reflection on the other?

Like many emerging technologies today where designers and users experiment to find helpful applications, the earliest railroads were more a novelty and tourist attraction than a practical transportation alternative. Reaching speeds of thirty miles per hour, one lady wrote in 1827, "It really appeared like flying."

However, the railway quickly demonstrated economic potential, for example, by increasing the tonnage of coal transport from Pennsylvania to New York City from 365 tons per year prior to the railroad to 123,000 tons per year in 1833. Libraries play an important role in demonstrating new technologies, even when the computer application or virtual reality experience seems more like a novelty. Library staffers play a vital part in collaborating with the whole community as a way to encourage innovation and entrepreneurship—and solve problems using these new tools.

Some libraries mistake adding or focusing on technology as an automatic means for people to tap into creative potential. This is not true. Technology is not the same as creativity. It is what you do with the technology that makes it a tool for creativity. "While technology can often be exciting to use, digital tools are just that, tools that can support a person's learning and ability to be creative," says Carly Reighard, assistant branch manager at the Abington branch, Harford County (MD) Public Library.

Librarians are in a leadership position. They can offer opportunities to kindle a person's creativity and sense of discovery with—or without—digital technology. Susan Neuman and Donna Celano, researchers and the authors of *Giving Our Children a Fighting Chance: Poverty, Literacy, and the Development of Information Capital*, observed library services in action for over fifteen years. A recent study by Neuman, Wong, and Tanya Kaefer concluded that while nothing can precisely mimic the experience of an adult reading aloud to a child, "there are certain features in video that might enhance word learning, especially for children with limited vocabulary."[2] Their research conclusions demonstrate that a strong self-teaching aspect is part of new technologies, and therefore the role of the parent as first teacher, for example, changes when using these digital tools. Librarians can help parents with these changes.

"What better place than a library for parents and caregivers to find support, resources, and kind reassurance that we're all learning about technology together," asks Lisa Guernsey, author and director of the Early Education Initiative and the Learning Technologies Project in the Education Policy Program at New America. Research by organizations such as New America, the Erikson Institute, the Joan Ganz Cooney Center, and others suggests the extraordinary opportunity for library staff to promote a common-sense approach to technology and find the right balance. Liz Kostandinu, the manager of Inquire Within, a WQED-PBS educational collaboration with Pittsburgh neighborhood libraries, says, "Libraries are great partners because they are long-standing community anchors. We see library staff meeting people where they are, listening in order to understand what families want and need." Tamara Kaldor, associate director of Erikson's Technology in Early

FIGURE 11.1

Although more a novelty than a practical application, taking virtual reality to the Boys & Girls Club of Westminster is a popular collaboration activity.

Note: the user is "repairing" a Star Wars ship.

Photo: Courtesy of Carroll County (MD) Public Library

Childhood Center, adds, "It can be easy to get caught up in just thinking about technology as a new digital game and virtual reality, but technology is a tool for creativity. All children must have access to technology tools to support their inquiry and to make their ideas take form. Librarians are poised to offer a range of activities, high-tech and low-tech, as a springboard for curiosity and constructive focus."

OPPORTUNITIES ARE LIMITLESS

Train travel in the nineteenth century uprooted people from all regions and, just like going to a public library today, generated the opportunity to meet and connect with other people who might or might not be like them. The quality of the experience for railroad commerce and for passengers was precarious at first. Basic rules were set up in the mostly classless passenger cars: the tobacco-chewing peddler sat next to the mother with her baby, and the millionaire socialized with the barber. Libraries are similar, offering perfect spots for the mingling of everyone in a community, no matter what a person's background or role in life.

As the railroads expanded westward in the mid- and late nineteenth century, they created a corridor of commerce centering in the growth of railroad villages, towns, and cities. Individuals and localities experimented with their resources—from turning fine clay into pottery and china to developing iron-smelting furnaces. When the transcontinental railroad was completed

FIGURE 11.2

Pi Day to celebrate math attracts 149 people at the Cohocton (NY) Public Library in this village of 800 people.

Photo: Courtesy of Cohocton (NY) Public Library

in 1869, it created a travel route across the continental United States and opened the West to settlement and development. The project united the country geographically, economically, socially, and culturally.

FIGURE 11.3

Drawing on local volunteer expertise, such as business owners, retirees, and college students, libraries are upping the ante in their ability to offer fun and engaging activities on an unlimited number of topics, including history, beekeeping, and mathematics.

Photo: Courtesy of Cohocton (NY) Public Library

FIGURE 11.4

Teens at ImagineIF in Columbia Falls, Montana, use conductive Bare Paint, LEDs, and art supplies to create colorful works of electric art.

Photo: Courtesy of ImagineIF

Many of us have a default tendency or habit of focusing on what is wrong in a situation, but if we tap large or abstract ideas of life, such as acceptance, discernment, peace, harmony, respect, and helpfulness, we can stay in tune with the bigger picture. We can develop a habit and steady attitude of looking for what is right—we don't ignore problems and challenges, but we try to see the good in people and think about how to correct issues. This is the essence of creativity: the ability to expand how well we listen and respond to our patrons, increase problem-solving skills, and create new possibilities for how a library and community can transform and thrive together. "We can practice Value Added Thinking by making sure that we play our part in any group with a measure of 'smooth functioning' and grace. We go beyond what is expected of us, both in our duties and creative contributions. We learn to put the needs of the group above our personal needs," says Carl Japikse, author of *What's the Big Idea?*[3]

Big-picture or universal thinking suggests that if we do not have the skill for this kind of thinking, then no matter how many boxes we think "outside" of we remain in a box and continue to limit our thinking. Plato's story or allegory of the cave in his famous Socratic dialogue *The Republic* reminds us that there are two levels of the mind. The lower mind focuses on personal points of views, observations, and assumptions, which often creates misunderstandings, selfishness, and prejudice. By asking the right questions and learning to ponder in a way to get good results, we can expand our thinking skills. We have the potential for higher-level thinking in order to tap universal ideas of harmony, benevolence, and goodwill.

We can tap ideas on how to

- Move forward with a major fund-raising campaign—think abundance, goodwill, and gratitude!
- Deal with unanticipated front-page newspaper coverage over a book controversy—think forgiveness, understanding, and flexibility!
- Redesign an old library building to include collaborative learning spaces as well as quiet study areas—think curiosity, adaptability, and wisdom!
- Connect the library and the community in fresh ways—think harmony, responsiveness, and dedication to the greater good!
- Bring out the best in a library curmudgeon who happens to be an elected official in your district—think patience and cheerfulness!
- Stay focused on the library as a means to enlighten humanity and help it grow—think innovation and creativity!

Henry Ford, like Tesla and others, had the ability to tap big ideas and download them into something constructive. "An even and flowing foundation of energy, a vivid and boundless imagination, a marvelous instinctive knowledge of mechanisms, and a talent for organization. These are the qualities that center in Mr. Ford,"[4] said Thomas Edison. Ford and his team pulled off a marketing coup by successfully replacing the Model T—which was out-of-date but beloved—with the Model A, which was far more popular, affordable, reliable, and efficient.

Henry Ford and others in the early twentieth century illustrate another example of tapping creativity and using big-picture thinking. By designing an inexpensive, high-quality automobile that many families could afford, the auto industry opened up another frontier for individual, convenient, and quick traveling experiences. Right timing is a key element in tapping the creativity needed to develop and implement projects. Ford and other early automobile engineers had impeccable timing as they observed the opportunities to replace travel by passenger trains with travel by automobiles. The tremendous independence and freedom to travel near and far offered by the automobile was above and beyond what passenger trains provided. Like the railroads in the nineteenth century, the affordable car upped the ante in the next century for mobility, creating the momentum for new societal growth, economically and culturally.

The character of Ford Motor's executive team in the early decades of the company—resilient, daring, and unruffled no matter what the crisis—reflected how they created a brilliant company from the ground up. Although libraries are not creating something from the ground up, we can apply the same

FIGURE 11.5

The library takes the lead to encourage community discussions with a fresh approach. How can the community proceed carefully but steadily to get unstuck from the past? Do Good Columbia initiative.

Photo: Courtesy of Richland (SC) Library

FIGURE 11.6

Library service is meant to be a group or community activity. An elected official helps celebrate the love of learning by participating in the library's Polar Express event.

Photo: Courtesy of Rochester Hills (MI) Public Library

qualities and characteristics—courageous, calm, dedicated, curious, generous, caring, helpful, and inspired—to refresh library service and customer experiences and thus become a magnet in the community for innovation.

Ford had a way of tapping people to join his lead team and connecting them to his vision of the greater good for humanity. He got them excited about the potential of building the first convenient, versatile, and widely affordable automobile. He turned a pricey, luxury machine into a necessity by making it inexpensive, practical, and easy to maintain. By combining mass production, a quality product, and high wages, he and his team helped to transform society economically, culturally, and socially. He offered a game plan for American business to grow and for society to improve. Can the library profession, including all types of libraries—public, school, academic, and special libraries—help our constituents develop a strong curiosity? Can we encourage individuals to become their best selves, to develop their genius? Can we encourage ourselves and our communities to ponder Ford's statement that "yesterday is past" and avoid relying on "last year's ideas"? Instead, can we help ourselves and others glean the message from the past and focus on working toward the future?

The versatility of the motorcar and Ford's ability to produce it on a huge scale changed a plaything into an efficient method for greater freedom of travel at the right price. Taking road trips and traveling across the country to visit national parks, scenic byways, and out-of-the-way attractions became popular. Today's driver packs up a smartphone, computer tablet, Wi-Fi capability, and a GPS system to help navigate. Gas stations, quality hotel chains, restaurants, and an outstanding highway system help us stay connected, safe, and comfortable while driving from city to city and town to town. The modern automobile offers a reliable, air-conditioned, easy-to-maneuver, 150-plus horsepower machine with many safety and comfort options, such as forward-collision warning, Bluetooth connectivity for hands-free phone use, a backup camera, blind-spot monitoring, height-adjustable lumbar support seating, heated seats and steering wheel, and other conveniences.

Ford said of his revolutionary first mass-produced car, "The Model T was a pioneer. It had stamina and power. It was the car that ran before there were good roads to run on. It broke down the barriers of distance in rural sections and brought people in those sections closer together."[5] Prior to the Model T other automobiles, ranging from the Packard steam carriage to the Daimler motor car and the Jenatzy electric car, were too expensive for the average family to purchase. Many of the early vehicles broke down frequently—in part due to bad roads. A soldier in World War I in France described the reliability and durability of the Model T: "When we struck a big hole filled with mud and water and dropped . . . she walked right out. Up half a mile, we smashed into another huge hole, and went right down to the chassis . . . to my extreme surprise I went up out of this hole and climbed up the side of it like a cat, and kept agoing."[6]

Libraries are in the midst of taking an adventurous road trip into new territory. We may get flak for something no other element of society is doing—encouraging people to think things through and embrace creativity in bigger

FIGURE 11.7

The idea of transcontinental travel by car captured the American imagination. Alice H. Ramsey, standing beside her auto in 1908, was the first woman to drive from New York to San Francisco. Along with three other women, none of whom knew how to drive, she packed up gas cans, bundled up for the weather, and drove 3,000 miles.

Photo by Bain News Service. Library of Congress

and bolder ways. Many people want to do what they know will work. For example, a publisher may encourage a children's author to write a book like *Harry Potter* because he or she knows it works. However, Harry Potter was a creative new idea that J. K. Rowling floated to numerous publishers who turned it down. Once someone recognized the genius of the Harry Potter stories and took a chance, *Harry Potter* transformed children's literature and young people's enthusiasm for reading.

Have you ever had the opportunity to enjoy viewing a master work of art in a museum exhibition? Were you struck by the artist's inspiration, such as the beauty and wholeness in Monet's *Reflections of Clouds on the Water-Lily Pond* or the strength and fortitude in Dali's *The Colossus at Rhodes*? There's a story about a visitor at the Hermitage Museum in St. Petersburg who was so awestruck by Rembrandt's *The Return of the Prodigal Son* that he stood for hours in front of the painting until a docent brought him a chair.

Although the ideal is to view the original painting, tapping the inspiration of the artist can still be powerful by looking at reproductions or online collections or art books. The more that libraries can help animate creativity and draw the best ideas from abstract thinking—to help generate innovation—the more libraries will fulfill the essence of service to the community. Some libraries circulate art reproductions, for example, and display the collection

FIGURE 11.8

Thomas Edison, John Burroughs, and Henry Ford enjoyed traveling together, including using Ford cars to go camping in the national forests. John Burroughs, naturalist and author, was hesitant to adopt the automobile at first, but did so and enjoyed using the motorcar.

Photo: Library of Congress

around the library. This innovative service not only makes beauty and inspiration available for customers to experience during their library visits, but also gives them the opportunity to borrow the prints for their home or office.

If we take the time to absorb the living essence of master works of classical art, it can help us explore the ideas of goodwill, benevolence, forgiveness, wisdom, compassion, and other life forces that are found not only in paintings but in great literature, theater, movies, and music. The composer Claude Debussy helps us be aware that there is more to life than what we see physically: there is kindness, cheerfulness, and integrity. Beethoven inspires unity, harmony, and peace. Many libraries and communities are increasingly aware that the library is not only a place with stacks of books, fun programs, and new tech demonstrations. We are a place that can encourage the genius in all of us—no matter what our starting point is. This idea of promoting genius— bringing out the inner best in someone—is not a situation where a "genius" works alone; it is about library staff and community members working as a creative team—bringing out the best in each other.

Some people may scoff at a library's support of creativity and genius in fresh ways, so be prepared to explain what you want to do. This book only suggests ways to tap creative and innovative ideas. The opportunities are virtually unlimited because libraries are discovering ways to help communities innovate—not just through technology, not just to do something in a different way, but to activate creativity and animate life.

FIGURE 11.9

Many historic library buildings undergo renovations that reveal inspiring original art hidden under layers of paint applied over the years.

Photo: Courtesy of Enoch Pratt Free Library, Baltimore

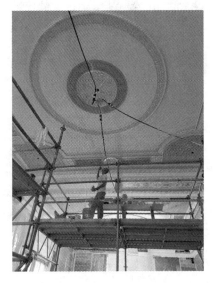

FIGURE 11.10

Music can add to the ambience of any program or event. A grand piano on wheels is poised to be played. During a building renovation a construction worker paused to greet patrons with his rendition of jazz and classical greats each morning. Enoch Pratt Free Library, Baltimore.

Photo: D. Stoltz

Can we be resilient, daring, and unruffled no matter what the situation—like the Ford Motor team? Yes! Can we activate curiosity in people to figuratively visit their storehouse of creativity—the national parks of ingenuity, scenic byways of innovation, and out-of-the-way attractions—in order to discover exciting ideas? Absolutely! Can we strive for the ideal to help libraries work toward the future and not get stuck in the past? Of course! The railroad and the automobile have reinvented themselves several times over and have helped define societal values in terms of self-fulfillment and abundance. Libraries, too, can avoid getting stuck in the past. Libraries have the potential to activate creativity in communities across the continent and change modern life irrevocably for the good.

NOTES

1. New York Public Library website, https://www.nypl.org/about/locations/jefferson -market.
2. Sri Ravipati, "Study: Preschoolers Learn Similarly for Digital and Print Books," *The Journal: Transforming Education through Technology*, May 9, 2017, https://thejournal .com/articles/2017/05/09/preschoolers-learn-similarly-for-digital-and-print-books.aspx.
3. Carl Japikse, *What's the Big Idea?* (Atlanta, GA: Enthea, 2006), 208–9.
4. Douglas Brinkley, *Wheels of the World: Henry Ford, His Company, and a Century of Progress 1903–2003* (New York: Viking, 2003), 363.
5. Richard Snow, *I Invented the Modern Age: The Rise of Henry Ford* (New York: Scribner, 2013), 321.
6. Snow, *I Invented the Modern Age*, 322.

AFTERWORD

It is up to each community (and its libraries) to "think through" how it can transform and thrive. The sky's the limit! The librarian of coming years can set this process in motion—inspiring individuals, groups, and organizations to learn, grow, and serve. It is not enough to wish, hope, or even plan for a library to be central to a community's success. Wishes need to be transformed into plans and plans need to be implemented. Library leaders who ask the right questions, take intelligent risks, and treasure the whole community are more likely to inspire others. Leadership begins with the library director and senior team working closely with other community sources of power, especially elected officials. Leadership implies that the organization as a whole is striving to activate creativity in ourselves and others. The goal of leadership—for all of us working in libraries—is to think and live in such a way as to bring out our personal inner best, the best of others, and the best of the community.

Robert Wack, physician and tech innovator, says, "I'm amazed at what my local public library is doing to support our efforts at MAGIC (Mid-Atlantic Gigabyte Innovation Collaboratory). I didn't understand at first when the library reached out. I'm beginning to see the dynamic role a library can play to encourage creativity and innovation and to help develop entrepreneurship." The entrepreneur Jason Stambaugh adds, "Libraries go far beyond providing information that people may or may not use. They can promote playful thinking, learning through doing, and the idea of pondering that can lead to innovation."

Confucius, a Chinese philosopher from the sixth century BC, was known for his popular aphorisms and his models of individual, governmental, and social well-being. From *Analectics*, a compilation of his teachings, book 1 features a conversation/lesson between a teacher and student. The student surmises that young people who respect their parents usually grow up to be mature and productive adults. The teacher responds: "Let young people show filial piety at home, respectfulness towards their elders when away from home; let them be circumspect, be truthful; their love going out freely towards all, cultivating good-will to men. And if, in such a walk, there be time or energy left for other things, let them employ it in the acquisition of literary or artistic accomplishments." This philosophy echoes Plato's thinking that children who learn to activate the good in their play are more likely to grow up with a vibrant, mature mind. Libraries can select copies of Confucius, Plato, Shakespeare, and Emerson that they find in their stacks and use them to start vibrant conversations with customers.

By implementing our finest skills, plans, and attributes, we can create a place for those working in libraries where confidence, ability, and right action increase. Join Emerson and scatter joy into our library work—and spark curiosity among ourselves and our community. In these ways, each library can transform and thrive—and help its community flourish.

Thinking Things Through

This is an activity to help facilitate a thinking process to take intelligent risks and to improve any type of challenge or opportunity.

My plan is:
- What elements of my library already exist that can support this plan? (For example, staff talents and community partnerships.)
- The needs of the library and community to be addressed with this plan are:
- How will this plan meet the needs of library customers? Describe the benefits.
- I'll contact the following staff members and/or partners to explore this plan:

1. _____

2. _____

3. _____

- Who else should be at the table? What will their roles/responsibilities be?
- What services are already in place? What will need to be created?
- What are the steps/activities that are needed to get this project established and services delivered? Create a time line to keep yourself on track.
- What do we need to spend money on? What sources of funding can be explored?
- What constitutes success? Who is defining success?

Adapted from Maryland State Library planning worksheet.

De Bono's Six Thinking Hats Exercise Adapted for Libraries

This exercise is meant to evoke different parts of our thinking abilities.

1. *White hat* (hat 1) = facts and objective information (scientist's white coat)

2. *Red hat* (hat 2) = elicit feelings, mood, and intuition ("heart" of feelings)

3. *Black hat* (hat 3) = why an idea may not work; inspire "devil's advocate" (black-robed judge)

4. *Yellow hat* (hat 4) = look for possible opportunities, benefits, and rewards (positive "sunny" outlook)

5. *Green* (hat 5) = find new, creative ideas (new shoots of grass)

6. *Blue* (hat 6) = "master" control hat to control thinking process and get overview and create summary (overarching sky)

Activity

1. Think of an issue or a problem you might want to solve. Or, think of an idea or a plan you'd like to implement. This can be work-related or not. Express it in one sentence.

2. Choose a hat to begin. Often, this is blue for how you should think about it. For example, what feelings (fears) need to be considered? What about future consequences? What do we need to learn first?

3. Go through all six hats and keep notes on your observations

   – *White*—what facts do I need and how do I get them?
   – *Red*—how do I feel about all of this?
   – Black—what are the risks? Worst-case scenario?
   – *Yellow*—what are all the possible advantages/benefits? What is the best possible outcome?
   – *Green*—what new approaches can I generate? How can I see this problem in a new way?
   – *Blue*—review and sum up what I have learned in this process. Next step?

Adapted from Six Thinking Hats by Edward de Bono

For more information, please contact Dorothy Stoltz, Carroll County (MD) Public Library, dstoltz@carr.org

Sample Issues for
de Bono's Six Thinking Hats Exercise

1. What is a real success for my library?

2. How can my library serve customers in ways to uplift, inspire, and enrich their lives?

3. How can my library overcome space limitations to create a makerspace or play-and-learn center while also offering quiet, contemplative spaces?

4. How can my library increase its ability to develop creative and innovative thinkers?

5. How can my library help "all boats rise"?

6. How can I connect entrepreneurs to my library?

7. How can I find individuals and groups who are doing innovative work and connect them to my library?

Sample Programming Statement

The purpose of library programming is to enlighten humanity. Programming supports the library's mission to inspire, educate, and enrich our community by offering opportunities for exploration, lifelong education, community engagement, and access to technology.

Staff are encouraged and expected to be creative and innovative to meet community needs. Programs incorporate a variety of interactions, such as one-on-one engagement, small group discussion or hands-on activities and large programs and events. Programs may be staff-led, presenter-led, or participant-led (i.e., self-directed program such as Make & Take craft program).

Programs should stimulate use of library resources by new as well as established library customers. They provide a unique opportunity to market and promote library services. Staff members determine the purpose of individual programs as part of the planning process, i.e., the audience (age, demographics, & size), community need being addressed, content, learning objectives, and outcomes.

Library staff should use the following criteria in planning library-sponsored programs:

- Alignment with current library strategic plan and mission
- Promotion of library collections and resources
- Timeliness and relevance of topic to community needs and interests
- Availability of funding
- Availability of programming space
- Promotional opportunities and publicity resource constraints
- Presenter background/qualification in content area
- Treatment of content for the intended audience
- Connection to other community activities

Programs may be held at any library facility or off-site.

Registration for programs may be required for planning purposes or when space is limited.

Some programs will require a fee for attendance.

Professional performers and guest presenters who possess specialized expertise may be selected for library programs.

The library may draw upon other community resources to develop cosponsored programs. Partners may include community agencies, organizations, businesses, educational and cultural institutions, and individuals.

The library may publicize programs under its sponsorship. In the case of cooperative publicity for cosponsored programs, the marketing department must approve final copy before the inclusion of the library's name or logo.

Library sponsorship of a program does not constitute an endorsement of the content of the program or the views expressed by presenters and participants.

Books, musical recordings, and other items may be sold at programs with prior approval by the library.

Professional performers and guest presenters *may not*:

- Promote or solicit for their business, group, or organization during their presentation. Business cards and/or brochures may be placed on a table in the room for audience pickup.
- Collect contact information, including, names, addresses, phone numbers, and e-mail addresses of audience members, without audience knowledge and approval.

Outside organizations may book a library meeting room based on established meeting room policy and regulations. In this case, the organization, business, or individual is responsible for booking the meeting room and doing their own publicity.

Adapted from Carroll County (MD) Public Library Program Handbook Appendix E

Sample Program Planning and Evaluation Guidelines

Library programs, events, and activities strive to spark curiosity and provide the highest-quality experience to inspire, educate, and enrich our community. *Staff work to develop interest-based, age-appropriate programs that reflect the needs of the community and support connected learning.* Programs incorporate a variety of types of interaction, such as one-on-one engagement, small group discussion or activities, and large programs and events.

These programs may be librarian-led, presenter-led, or participant-led.

Programs should stimulate the use of library resources by new as well as established library customers. This is a visible way to market and promote library services. Staff members determine the purpose of individual programs as part of the planning process; that is, they consider the audience (age, demographics, and size), the community need being addressed, and the content, learning objectives, and outcomes.

Research Your Community

Research should include identifying needs and interests, responding to trends, and knowing not just who you want to attract, but what will attract them. Depending on the program(s), formal and informal research methods and tools may be appropriate and useful, such as CCPL statistical databases; local, state, and national data; formal and informal library surveys; and conversations with individuals and community partners.

Programming Priorities

When designing and planning programs and activities, use these priority categories to guide your decision-making:

- Building Community—school readiness, social opportunities and skills, entrepreneur and business connections, citizenship, partnership events, entertainment

- Cultural Arts Literacy—literature, music, art, history, theater, philosophy
- Technology/STEM Literacy—science, technology, engineering, math

Planning Logistics

Asking questions and thinking things through can help in the program planning process. For example, program evaluation, formal or informal, should not be considered a stand-alone activity. It should rather be thought of as a set of linked tasks that are undertaken from the start to the end (and beyond) of a program. Consider planning questions, such as:

- How will the program meet the needs of the audience being served? Describe the benefits and desired impact.
- Has this program or activity been attempted previously? Who can share their expertise?
- Who else should be at the table? Do I need a program planning team? Will the team include community partners? What will their roles/responsibilities be?
- Remember to diversify your team as well as your audiences.
- What are the steps/activities that are needed to get the program planned and implemented? Create a time line to keep yourself on track.
- What will you need to spend money on? What sources of funding can be explored?
- How can you promote locally to ensure you're reaching target audiences? Can community partners help?
- What will success look like? How will you measure success? What tools/expertise (formal or informal) will you need to measure success?

Scheduling

Scheduling the right time and place for a program is an important part of planning. Consider community/library system/branch/department priorities when scheduling a program, such as staffing, branch needs, overall branch programming schedule, work time allowance, funding, national or community events and trends. Utilizing statistics of past programs can help determine season, day of week, and time for the most effective program.

Successful Implementation

The structures you and your team establish to support implementation of your programs, activities, and events will be an important factor in determining the success of your program. Structures include details such as staffing, room/location setup, announcement, presentation, and cleanup.

Implementation Logistics

Asking questions and thinking things through can help in the implementation process. Consider planning questions, such as:

- How will the program meet the needs of the audience being served? Describe the benefits and desired impact.
- Is the program feasible and realistic? Is the cost in staff time, supplies, and resources worth the investment?
- Has this program or activity been attempted previously? Who can share their expertise?
- Do I need a program planning team? Who else should be at the table? Will the team include community partners? What will their roles/responsibilities be?
- Will the program(s) appeal to a diverse audience?
- What are the steps/activities that are needed to get the program planned and implemented? Create a time line.
- Identify costs. What sources of funding can be explored?
- How can the program be promoted in the library service area to ensure reaching the target audiences? Can community partners help?
- What staff will set up the room and help the presenter as needed? What staff will introduce guest presenter, welcome participants, and promote other programs and services? Such as:
    - Upcoming programs in branch and/or system wide events
    - Library Friends group
    - Library card, other services

For programs with adult audiences:

- If this is a new presenter to the Library, who will observe the presenter's entire first program?

For programs with youth and children:

- Who will attend, observe, and assist for the duration of all programs?
- Debrief/self-evaluate the success of the program. How will staff celebrate the achievement of successfully implementing the program? Acknowledging and celebrating accomplishments are good for morale and help to propel staff to the next opportunity for program planning and implementation. Sharing program successes enables replication at other locations.

Measuring Success

What will success look like? How will staff measure success? What tools/expertise (formal or informal) will you need to measure success?

Post-Program Cost-Benefit Analysis

What worked well? What didn't work? What could you have done differently to have been more successful?

Depending on the program, compile a list of costs and benefits associated with the program. Consider the overall cost to hold a program - presenter fees, staff preparation time, marketing and promotion, meeting room space, program supplies, time that could have been spent on other tasks, etc. The benefits include increased learning for the customer, increased community collaboration, program statistics, increased door counts, awareness of other library services, and goodwill. The planning team can compare costs and benefits to determine if the benefits outweigh the costs. If so, then the rational decision is to go forward with program. If not, a review of the project is warranted to see if adjustments can be made to either increase benefits and/or decrease costs in order to make the program viable. If not, the program should be abandoned.

Consider evolving customer needs.

As an example of how to determine needs, a short survey such as:

- I learned something I can share [with others] [with my children]
  Agree—Neutral—Disagree

- I feel more confident [about this topic] [with technology] [with this activity]
  [to help my children learn]
  Agree—Neutral—Disagree

- What more can the library do for you and your family?

Program Costs

Program costs may include guest presenter or performer fees and travel expenses, program supplies, and light refreshments. If grant funds are used, ensure that all expenditures adhere to the grant guidelines.

Adapted from Carroll County (MD) Public Library Program Handbook

Sample Event Planning and Special Programs Checklist

6–10 Months Ahead

- ☐ Estimate costs, finalize budget, get approval as needed to determine appropriate budget(s)
- ☐ Is guest presenter/topic better suited for within a branch or outside of the branch
- ☐ Check with branch manager(s) who can offer insights about community interest
- ☐ Check with human resources department to determine the eligibility for staff contact hours and the logistics for staff attending
- ☐ Once date, time, and location are confirmed, event coordinator will e-mail the director's staff and materials manager as a heads-up and appropriate branch staff as a heads-up
- ☐ If the program will take place at a branch:
  - Branch manager helps determine who the branch contact person should be to work with administrative contact person
  - Determine who will book the meeting room or make plans for a program on the library floor

- ☐ If the program will take place outside a branch:
  - Who should be the library contact person to work with the community venue staff?

- ☐ Decide on time and date
- ☐ Get written contracts as appropriate
- ☐ Determine who will input publicity and when; whether the program can be included in the library newsletter; determine flyers, signage
  - Work with your marketing department liaison to arrange for any special publicity needs, such as press releases, social media, special distribution, and inclusion in e-mail blasts

- Work with your marketing department liaison to determine signage for book sale/author signing tables

2–6 Months Ahead

☐ Arrange for speaker/guest presenter needs, hotel, transportation, if applicable

☐ Work with materials management department if program requires the purchase of books (If a large crowd is expected, consider ordering titles in bulk; if event is small, work with author/presenter to supply books for purchase.)

☐ Send an e-mail to invite staff to sign up to work the event as event "helpers," in which case the event will be considered work time
  - Depending on the event, the e-mail invitation will specify how to register; for example, if the registration includes a book and/or a meal, a registration code may be given to waive the cost
  - Depending on the event, the e-mail invitation can be sent to branch and/or team-specific staff, other selected staff, or to all staff as appropriate

☐ If an event requires ticket sales or registration requirements outside of the norm, contact both the marketing and finance departments

☐ Determine who will be responsible for on-site needs, such as room setup, greeters, ushers, food preparation, and presenter introduction, other

☐ Will the event involve a vendor or food preparation? If so, fill out appropriate forms and submit to the health department within at least two weeks of the event

☐ Administration, branch contacts, guest presenter, and partners finalize plans

☐ Review/finalize budget, tasks, and tentative time line
  - Send finance department the budget information and submit any necessary purchase requisitions
  - Give a heads-up as to how to expect payment; for example, credit card, invoices, employee reimbursement form

☐ Give estimate of guests expected to cater or prepare food, if applicable

One Month Ahead

☐ Confirm staff for on-site needs, such as setup, greeters, ushers, food preparation, presenter introduction, and book sales, other

☐ Contact program participants, confirm participation

☐ Complete list of contents for event program/agenda if applicable

☐ Determine setup needs and design a plan for who will do what

☐ Review script/time line/program details

☐ Review with finance department how to secure a cash box and credit card machine if needed for the day of the event and ensure that staff know how to use the credit card machine

☐ Plan for reserved seating as needed

☐ Confirm speaker/presenter needs, audiovisual, other

One Week Before the Event

☐ Confirm with team for last-minute details

☐ Confirm staff arrival time

☐ Confirm staff assignments such as setup, greeters, ushers, food preparation, presenter introduction, book sales, other

☐ Finalize catering guarantee, refreshments

Event Day

☐ If the event takes place off-site, the event coordinator will meet with the on-site manager to work through any last-minute details and set up a way to communicate throughout the event

☐ Event coordinator will ensure that all staff are aware of their assigned tasks

☐ Provide copies of attendee list to all necessary staff

☐ Acknowledge staff and partners

☐ Take photos

After the Event

☐ Following an event (which had paid registration), combine marked attendance sheets (if there are more than one) and give to finance to mark the attendance on their online list

☐ Follow up to be sure all invoices are received by finance, submit any expenses for reimbursement (for example, an author's train ticket), follow up with any hotel or other vendors for the final bill, return the cash boxes, return any other equipment borrowed from anywhere else, and return unsold books

☐ Upload photos to cloud storage and share on social media

☐ Send a "thank you" to those involved (if deemed appropriate)

Adapted from Carroll County (MD) Public Library Program Handbook

Shakespeare: Interrogating the Text

CECILIA RUBINO

When approaching a monologue or a scene from a Shakespeare play, here are a few possible first steps:

- Read the text aloud for sense. Ask yourself what's the story of the speech or the scene and boil down the essence of what it's about into a short phrase.
- Paraphrase the text line by line, that is, read a line from Shakespeare and then put it into your own words.
- Scan the text for rhythm and meter. Iambic pentameter or blank verse (which Shakespeare is often writing in) is made up of five pairs of unstressed/ stressed syllables. Look for this "pulse" and then identify where there are shifts in the meter or additional syllables.
- Look up words you may not know and/or research the pronunciation of a word if you have any questions.
- Pay attention to the first word and the last word of the verse line (especially the last word!).
- Find the verbs and then the operative or scintillating words.
- What's the scaffolding of the argument in the text? Pay attention to the use of antithesis and rhetoric.
- Take note of alliteration, assonance, repetitions, lists, and rhymes in the text.
- Investigate the "given circumstances," which could include:

  - *Who*: Delve into the evidence in the text about your character's personal history and their relationship to other characters. What is their heart's desire, the object of their passion, and what do they want or need in the scene?
  - *Where*: The physical and social environment of the scene. Be specific!
  - *When*: The time of day, year, and if necessary, the historical period.
  - *What*: What is the main event of the scene or monologue and how does it connect to the main event of the play?
  - *Why*: Delve into specifying and justifying your characters' choices.

- Work the first beat. Ground yourself in the physical. What has just happened? What trigger question is your character responding to?
- Physically explore the images in the text.
- Create a physical score for the scene or monologue. What is your character doing from moment to moment? Explore a range of physical choices and the stakes in the scene. Go big, dare to be extravagant, and then reground yourself in authenticity.
- Remember! All the preparation is just the groundwork, it's fertilizer. Finally, "the readiness is all"; you must be present and in the moment—think, feel, and speak at the same time. Also remember, when speaking Shakespeare's verse, that you will need to let the words "trip off your tongue," so you may need to allow yourself to think, feel and speak with a certain alacrity.

Suggested Resources

- American Library Association
- Aspen Institute
- Center for the Future of Libraries
- Erikson Institute
- Global Family Research Project
- Harwood Institute of Public Innovation
- New America

Suggested Reading

Aristotle. *Aristotle Nicomachean Ethics*. Translated by Joe Sachs. Bemidji, MN: Focus Publishing, 2002.

de Bono, Edward. *Creativity Workout: 62 Exercises to Unlock Your Most Creative Ideas*. Berkeley, CA: Ulyssses, 2008.

———. *Lateral Thinking: Creativity Step by Step*. New York: Harper Perennial, 2015.

———. *Six Thinking Hats*. New York: Hachette Book Group, 1999.

Emerson, Ralph Waldo. *Essays: First and Second Series*. Germany: Jazzybee Verlog, (2017).

Japikse, Carl. *What's the Big Idea?* Atlanta, GA: Enthea, 2006.

O'Neill, John J. *Prodigal Genius: The Life of Nikola Tesla*. Kempton, IL: Adventures Unlimited, (2008).

Plato. *Republic*. Translated by Benjamin Jowett, Introduction by Elizabeth Watson Scharffenberger. Barnes & Noble Classics, 2005.

Shakespeare, William. *The Norton Facsimile The First Folio of Shakespeare*. New York: W.W. Norton and Company, (1996).

ABOUT THE AUTHORS

GAIL GRIFFITH recently retired from a long career in public libraries, including twenty-five years as the deputy director of the Carroll County (MD) Public Library. She has also consulted with libraries around the United States on planning and training projects. Griffith is the recipient of the Maryland Library Association Award for distinguished service to Maryland libraries, and she coauthored (with Paula Singer) *Succession Planning in the Library: Developing Leaders, Managing Change* for the American Library Association.

JAMES KELLY is the associate director for operations at the Frederick County (MD) Public Libraries. Over the past twenty years his work has involved listening to and empowering people, and fostering individual and community growth. He is past president of the Maryland Library Association's Leadership Development Division and past chair of the Maryland Library Leadership Institute Task Force. His training experience lies in mentoring, mindful leadership, strategic planning, organizational culture, and core values development.

MUFFIE SMITH is the director of human resources for the Carroll County Public Library in Maryland. She has worked in public libraries for forty-three years. Her first seventeen years were spent working in progressively more responsible positions in the circulation department of the Towson Branch of the Baltimore County Public Library. The remainder of her time has been spent in her current position. She remains dedicated to exceptional customer service.

LYNN WHEELER has been executive director of the Carroll County (MD) Public Library since 2004; the library's circulation and programming per capita are often ranked first in Maryland. Wheeler has previously served in a number of capacities in the library and education fields, including a stint as assistant director for human resources and branch library services at the Baltimore County Public Library, and working at Library Systems and Services Inc. and the College of Information Studies, University of Maryland. She serves on numerous state and county boards.

INDEX